The North Bay Narrative

North Bay village, school house front center, circa 1914.

The North Bay Narrative

by

Walter Staples

Peter E. Randall Publisher
Portsmouth, New Hampshire
1998

Printed in the United States of America

Design: Jack Pollard

Peter E. Randall Publisher
Box 4726, Portsmouth, NH 03802

Library of Congress Cataloging-in-Publication Data

Staples, Walter, 1913-
The North Bay narrative / by Walter Staples.
p. c m .
ISBN 0-914339-70-2 (alk. paper)
1. North Bay (Nfld.)—History. 2. North Bay (Nfld.)—Biography. 3. Frontier and pioneer life—Newfoundland —North Bay. I. Title.
F1124.5.N67S83
1998 971.8—dc2l

98-31488
CIP

A quote (via Jim) from Kenneth Robert's *Arundel*...

"Almost anything in the world is readily forgotten after ten years. After the passage of fifty years a happening so fades into the mists of antiquity that little is known about it except by those who took part in it; and that little is mostly wrong."

Trudy,

(603) 323-7973

Walter Staples

North Bay Narrative

sent inquiry about distribution, didn't hear back.

To Jill ☐ **URGENT**

Date 6/11 Time 11:30 (A.M.) P.M.

WHILE YOU WERE OUT

From Doug Rooks

of

Phone

Area Code Number Ext.

Fax

Area Code Number

Telephoned	
Came to see you	
Returned your call	

Please Call	
Wants to see you	
Will call again	

Message

DID GET THE MANUSCRIPT

Signed

Quill Corporation 1-800-789-1331 #7-92001 Reorder No.

Contents

Acknowledgments

Without the diary of Josiah Farrell that his daughter, Pearl, typed and added to, and of which Ernest Farrell sent me a copy, the memories recalled and shared with him by descendants of the pioneer settlers of North Bay would never have become a book.

Ernest Farrell's many informative, hand written letters in response to my questions explained in detail a way of life and the people of the remote village; and conversations with Jack and Jean Farrell, Percy and Violet Taylor, Max and Hilda Strickland, Arthur Farrell and his daughter Verna Billard, provided information about how the second and later generations adapted to the great changes that took place as they grew up. Verna Billard provided old pictures of people who lived at North Bay, Ernest Farrell pictures of boats and buildings.

The guiding and fishing activities since 1930 result from observations during my own annual trips to fish for Atlantic salmon on the LaPoile river, from the knowledge, expertise, experience, and camaraderie of the guides that made each trip one to remember: head guide, Alec Chant, his brothers Sidney and Garland, Lewis Bond and Reggie Chant, the River Guardian, Phil Bond, and Alec's wife Eilene.

Though Duncan Smith died only two years after having invited me to bring annual salmon fishing parties to his cabin at Salmon Hole pool on the LaPoile, that first year with "Dunc," Carl Ross, Doctor Foley, and Dick Goodell was the beginning of a long and memorable adventure, and resulted in this book.

And deep appreciation to my wife Virginia whose editing corrected my many errors and typos.

Preface

As a student member of Donald B. MacMillan's sixteenth Arctic expedition, helping a Newfoundland crew catch, split, and salt pack cod in the hold and on the deck of their sixty-foot, two-masted wooden sailing schooner—one of a fleet of a hundred such that once numbered a thousand fishing along the coast of Labrador—I became interested in these sturdy ships and their hardy crews.

Like true Maine farmers, Newfoundlanders are inclined to be taciturn, particularly in the presence of foreigners. It was after ten or more annual salmon fishing trips to the La Poile River, and during an in-camp day of high water and windblown rain, that I learned from talking with the guides that such fishing boats had been built by rugged pioneer families at the remote village where this river enters saltwater at the head of North Bay. From that time on I undoubtedly made a nuisance of myself, asking questions in interviews and in letters, many of them personal, of the present generations of those pioneers, some of whom had been involved in the later years of boat building at North Bay.

Once involved, it seemed I had to learn all that I could about these pioneer families, the land they settled, their homes and families, and the when and how of the boats they built. The twentieth-century history of the village of North Bay included sixty years of active and profitable boat building and guiding moose and caribou hunters and salmon fishermen, the melding occupations both dependent on the natural resources of the area. But I also wanted to look at the effect of modern civilization on the continued existence of North Bay and similar outport villages.

The North Bay Narrative may echo circumstances that

Newfy fishing boat at Cut Throat Harbor, Labrador, 1937.

occurred in other small and remote harbor villages along the south shore of Newfoundland, villages located at the head of remote and shallow bays and bypassed by weekly ferries and all but the smallest fishing boats of local origin. Like North Bay, these villages will soon cease to exist as permanent year-round settlements.

Donald B. MacMillan Arctic Expedition

On the *Gertrude L. Thebaud*, Cut throat Harbor, Labrador, 8/13/37 from my diary:

.... Pete [Peter Stengel] called that the fishermen were going out in their powerboat (fifteen-foot wooden boat with single cylinder in-board motor) to haul the nets. We had already asked them to take us along—and they were stopping for us.

Newfoundland fishing boat "down north along the Labrador."

Pitching cod from deck to cutting table

A layer of fish, a layer of salt. Cod stacked on the deck after the hold was filled. Cook washes clothes on stern.

It was interesting to haul the nets in spite of the fact that we got only a few quintal of fish—but when we finished hauling the last net we did some jigging and caught cod as fast as we could haul them in.

One of the men asked if I would send him a picture (I had taken several) if they came out well. I promised and asked him to write his name and address—he couldn't read or write; but as he spelled it, I wrote the following:

Patrick Broomfield
St. Brends, Bona Vista Bay
Newfoundland.

The names of the eight schooners anchored in this [Cut-throat] harbor are as follows: *Louisa AM, Rita Windsor, Hazel Pearl, Louisa T Churchill, Hubert Brian, E.J. Hennessy, A&R Martin, W. J. Ellisson.*

I enjoyed talking with one old skipper as we came in from the last haul. I don't suppose that he could read or write. He had worked a year in New York City; but the cod of the Labrador coast called him again and he returned. Like the New Englander and his farm, so the Newfoundlander and his schooner. Neither will admit it; but neither would be satisfied doing anything else, even if he could.

Walter Staples

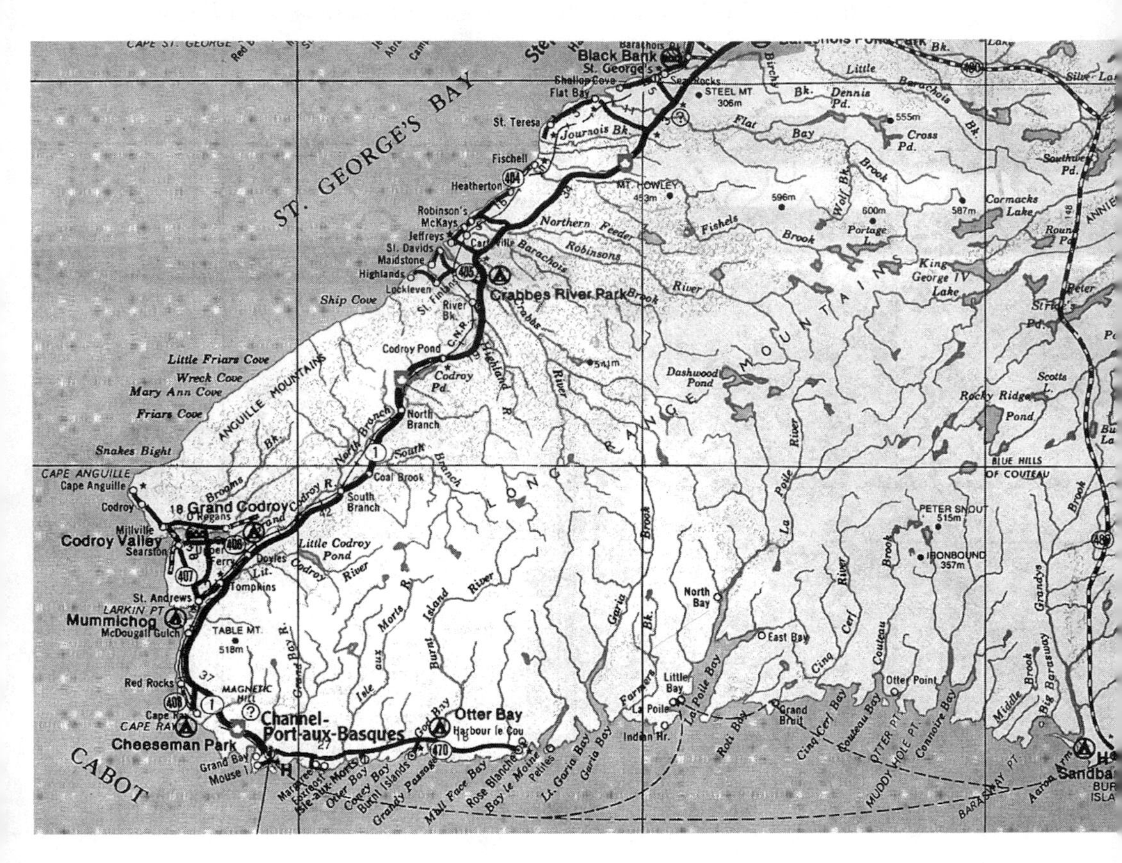

Map of southwest coast of Newfoundland. North Bay is at right of lower center.

1

The La Poile Bay and La Poile River

The western end of the south coast of Newfoundland, from Port aux Basques to Burgeo and beyond, is one of huge, wave-washed rocks and deep-water bays and coves, and easterly abrupt thousand-foot headlands rise from the coast. The earlier fishermen, French, Portuguese, and Spanish, had built in the small protected harbors. The French village names persist although the English, after a series of defeats and victories, eventually took possession of all but two islands far to the east. Even then however, the English allowed the French to continue fishing the south shore under treaty rights until the French built homes and villages and lobster processing plants there in violation of the agreement. By then the French population had reached an alarming number and the treaty rights were terminated.

The high inland mountains creep closer to the ocean easterly from Port aux Basques. The bays are deeper and longer past Isle-aux-Morts, Rose Blanche, and Petites. The first high and steep headland pounded by ocean waves rises between La Poile village and the nine-mile-long La Poile Bay, with its wide North East Arm.

Half a mile wide where East Arm joins it, the north branch narrows between higher and steeper mountains the remaining six miles to where the La Poile River meets the tidewater. Though heavily forested with spruce, fir, and yellow birch, the mountain walls are so steep and the soil so thin, that great slides often start from heavy rains, leaving a ribbon of bare rock from the mountaintop to where a pile of roots, trees, and the sparse vegetation is piled in the edge of the bay. Such swaths, in various stages of regeneration, run parallel to the many streams originating in the

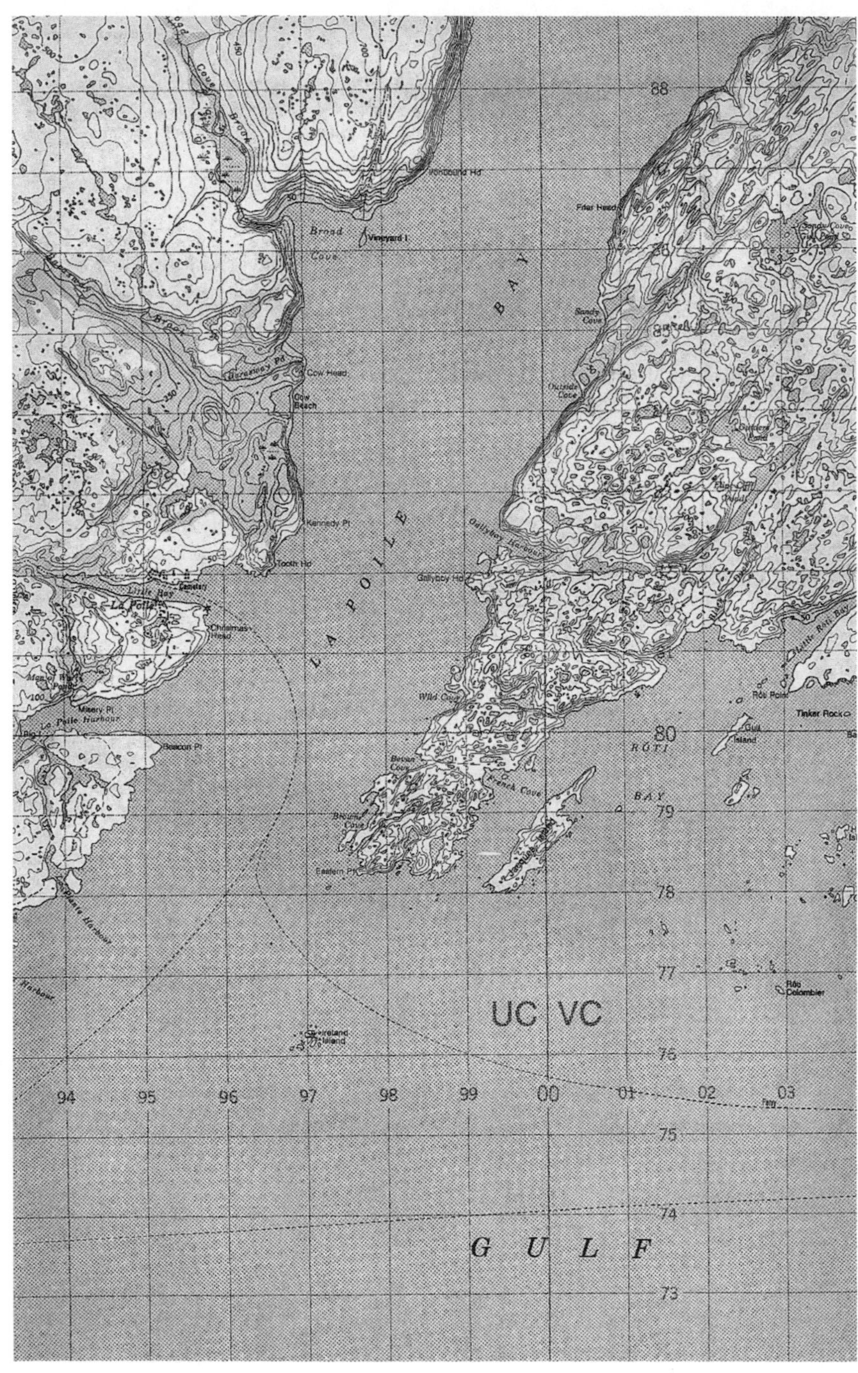

Map of LaPoile Bay.

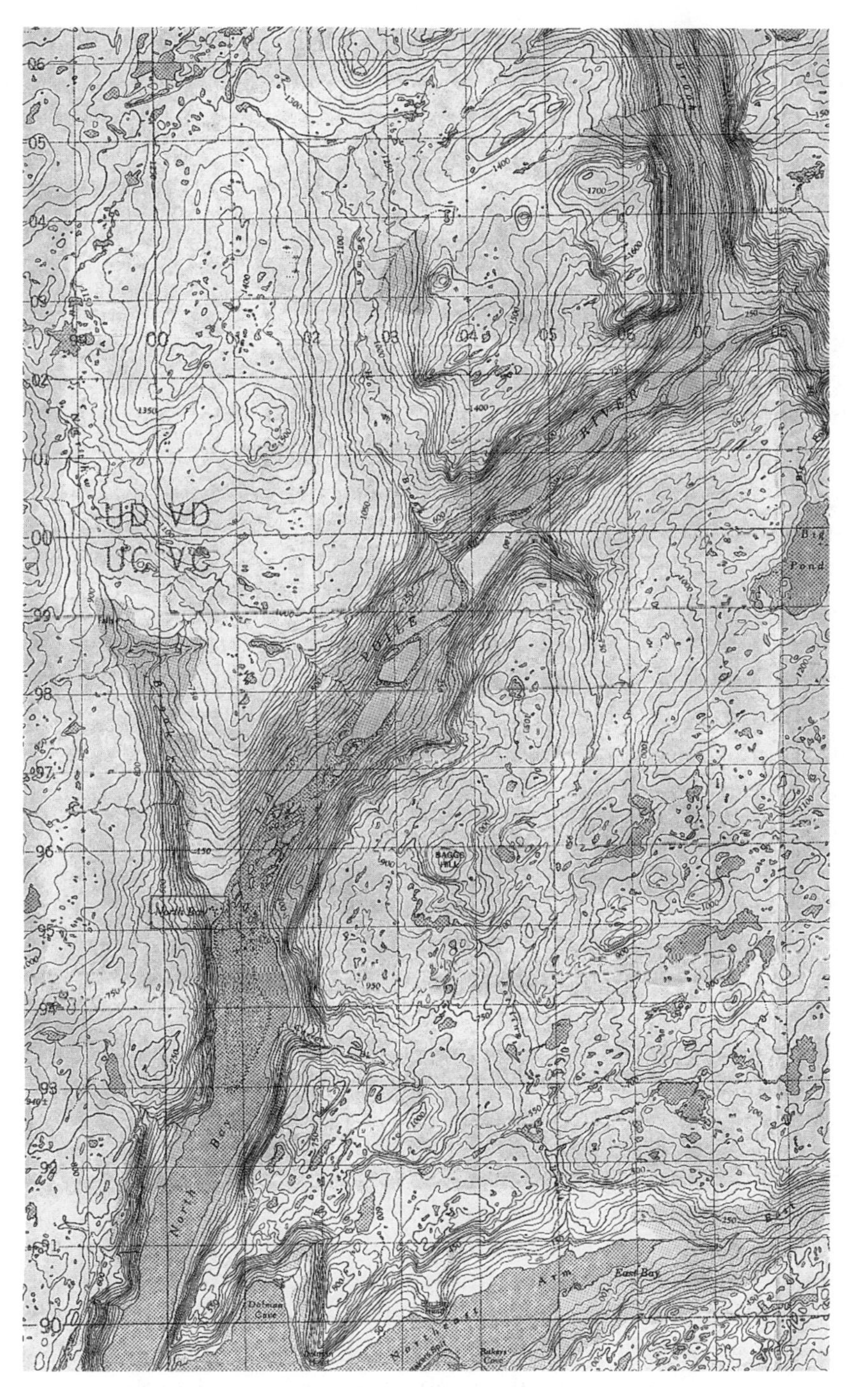

Map of North Bay and the LaPoile River.

highland that bounce from rock to rock in a thousand flumes of white water falling up to two thousand feet to join the bay.

From the bay, the mountaintops appear barren; but to those who have climbed there, they are a tangle of water bush and stunted spruce, thick enough in places to support a man walking three feet or more above their roots, dominated by outcropping rock, lakes and ponds, and an occasional canyon where the forest may provide protection for caribou and moose, black bear, ptarmigan, bobcat, lynx, fox, and Arctic hare.

At the head of the bay the La Poile River enters at both sides of the valley, having split some two miles above, forming a series of forested islands and grassy meadows separated by rock-bedded high-water crossings. Here the mountains, creased with small valleys and feeder streams, delay the morning sun on the pools and bring an early-afternoon shade to those who cast their salmon flies.

The fishermen who named the protective harbors along the south coast were almost nomadic. Their villages consisted of a few houses to provide a haven for their boats and crews during the migrating fish season, and a place to salt, dry, and store their catch until quantities were supplied to load for markets that might be across the sea. Harbors where ships could be repaired and stores replenished, where a family might be waiting, did not require surrounding timber or depend on wildlife for food. They likely burned coal for fuel and brought the boards for their temporary houses with them rather than cut logs for cabins.

The settlers from the north and northwest coast and from the inland rivers and bays, where some degree of agriculture could be practiced on less formidable land, added an active industry of boatbuilding to satisfy a strong demand by those who participated in the extensive cod fishing "down north along the Labrador." The industry required timber; and as the available timber was cut in their vicinity, the boatbuilding families migrated to bays and valleys where the virgin timber was still available. Their belongings were limited to a stove and essential housewares, along with hand tools, pit saws, and ropes. A man might even take his house apart to transport on his boat with him to a new location, or in some shorter moves, such as a mile or two up the bay, might tow it behind his boat on a raft to relocate closer to suitable boat-building timber and to another such "pioneer."

This migration of boat builders, like caterpillars extending their forage area, was creeping along the south shore of Newfoundland in the late 1800s, down past Otter Bay, Burnt Island, Petites, Indian Harbor, and La Poile. Some families moved into Northwest Cove in La Poile Bay behind a small island at the mouth of Barasway Brook—nearly opposite where Northeast Arm and East Bay enter La Poile Bay—and one family moved to a small protected shelf of land in Dolman Cove, just inside and on the north shore of Northeast Arm.

2

La Poile

By 1900 Thomas Le Sellieur had an active business in a large two-story building on the west side of Little Harbor, just west of the high headland marking the entrance to La Poile Bay. A single man, he had emigrated from the Jersey Isles some twenty years before, acquired the property three miles east of West Point, a village of fourteen families, and started buying and processing cod and other fish. For a while he also processed whales during their annual migration.

He built a sturdy wharf in front of his building. It extended to deep water of the harbor and could accommodate oceangoing vessels, the local freighters, and whaling ships, as well as boats of the local fishermen and lobstermen.

He built his own home near the building and kept a lady housekeeper; but he never married.

The second floor of the large building, intended as a warehouse and storage area, soon became a store—a combination grocery, clothing store, pharmacy, hardware shop, furniture store, lumber yard, marina, in fact a general store stocking anything that the local population might require. The "local" population included dozens of small villages both east and west. His nearest competition, Port aux Basques, was more than fifty miles to the west, and none other existed for hundreds of miles to the east along the south shore of Newfoundland.

To provide the labor necessary to carry on his many activities, Le Sellieur sent back to the Jersey Isles for relatives, friends, and people needing work who were willing to try life in a new country. He undoubtedly financed their transportation and the homes he built for them when they arrived. With limited space available close to the store and his house, after only seven houses were built nearby, additional houses were constructed on the rocky slope across the harbor. These became the village of La Poile.

La Poile grew to be a thriving community of more than two hundred families with Le Sellieur's store at its heart. His customers were from the dozens of small villages within rowing or sailing distance. The residents of these villages were primarily fishermen and boatbuilders. While all fishermen could and often did build their own rowboats and dories, and the boatbuilders fished for cod, salmon, and lobsters for their own food supply, the nature of their livelihood influenced the location of their homes. The fishermen chose the small protected harbors near the ocean and built their houses on the bare rocks to be near their fishing grounds. The boatbuilders went deep into the long bays to the mouth of the rivers that flowed through wide valleys filled with mixed growth forest of spruce, fir, and yellow birch. They built their big houses in the shadows of the mountain on banks of soil that would support a garden and grow grass for a cow and

LaPoile village and headland.

sheep; and they trapped and hunted wild animals and birds to provide variety to their diets.

Thomas Le Sellieur, with the commercial contacts he had with the major trading centers of Newfoundland, Port aux Basques, Saint John's, mainland Canada, and the United States—in fact, with world ports—must have been well informed. Such matters as the 1892 Saint John's fire, the building of the narrow-gauge railway between Saint John's and Port aux Basques, and the changes in the French treaty rights affecting the south shore must have influenced his trading and transportation requirements. But none of these important affairs seems to have been cause for concern or even discussion among the outport villagers. Their concerns were limited to fishing and boatbuilding: in short, to survival.

3

The Pioneers

In 1875, at age twenty-three, John Strickland was living in the small village of West Point on the southwest coast of Newfoundland. The European demand for salted cod was being met by Newfoundland fishermen plying coastal waters and a growing fleet of nearly a thousand ships sailing north each spring to follow the cod migration along Labrador's coast.

Like other men of West Point, John not only fished when the cod were running and when the salmon returned to the spawning rivers of their ancestors, he at times also rowed his boat the three miles easterly to La Poile and worked at the plant where fish were processed, salted, and shipped to a number of world ports. He worked at catching and processing whales during the season when they migrated along the coast. And when no seasonal work was available, he built boats–the only means of local transportation–for himself, and helped others who were less adept, less able, or less willing to perform such intricate construction.

Even as a teenager, John had rowed around the headland into La Poile Bay, passed East Bay, and on up to North Bay, a total of nine miles, to the mouth of the La Poile River to fish and hunt in the wide valley between the steep mountains. Now he built a small log cabin on the high bank behind the westerly side of the smaller branch of the river, a place to spend the nights during his more frequent trips and longer stays, while catching fish or hunting caribou to take back to La Poile or West Point to sell.

He married Fanny Herridge, of Harbor Le Cou, and moved there, making a living as a fisherman. He and Fanny had nine children, four boys and five girls: Alice, May, Andrew, Frank,

Archibald, John, Loulea, Julia, and Rachel. As the boys got into their teens, John took his sons on frequent trips to the cabin at the head of North Bay.

Frank and Andrew adapted readily to pioneer life. They became aware of the natural resources of timber suitable for boat-building and of the cod and salmon runs in the bay and the river. Andrew, in particular, developed an affinity for the area that was akin to guardian or even owner; and when in 1891 his father left on a fishing boat for Labrador and did not return, sixteen-year-old Andrew, with his younger brother Frank, continued seasonal fishing and lobster trapping along the shore. They made frequent visits to the few families, including the Thomas Farrells, who had moved to East Bay from the West Point, and the John Taylor family, living at Northwest Cove three miles or so up the bay.

With their mother and five younger siblings to support, Andrew and Frank were hard pressed, even with considerable support from relatives and neighbors, to feed the family. After about four years, with Andrew not twenty, they decided to move the family to North Bay. Alice had married. John, May, and Archibald stayed with an aunt in Harbor Le Cou; but Loulea, Julia, Rachel, and their mother took their meager belongings to North Bay. Though crowded in the small log cabin their father had built seventeen years earlier, they spent the next several summers at North Bay.

Andrew, with Frank's help, set the spruce sills of his new house on large and readily available rocks a foot or more above the soggy soil and framed it with local fir, sized by ax and adze. They bartered boards for roof and siding with West Point village boat-builders, who pit sawed their own board requirements, in return for sixty-foot spruce logs fit for masts. These were plentiful and easily accessible at North Bay, and beside the river into which they could be felled for transportation to the head of the bay, then towed behind a rowboat to their destination.

With his two-story, six-room house now built, and space for his mother and three sisters, Andrew married Martha Taylor, daughter of John Taylor of Northwest Cove, and brought his bride to the new home.

Frank had visited the Thomas Farrells at East Bay regularly during his trips to North Bay over the years, his interest as much in their daughter Annie as with her six brothers. There would be room in Andrew's house, and before winter passed he could have a home of his own. Annie had undoubtedly looked forward to leaving her position as older sister and perennial baby sitter to six brothers. Frank's visits sparked a romance now ready to be fulfilled, and soon they were married. Annie helped Frank dig a shallow cellar and build a large two-story home at North Bay, not far from Andrew's.

There were no permanent neighbors in the six-mile stretch between North Bay and East Bay. Two hunter-trapper Indians temporarily lived in, or at least used, a crude log hut on the southeast coast of the bay, not far from where the Stricklands settled at North Bay. They and individual hunters who wandered the nearby mountains occasionally visited the village. They were friendly but aloof. They never caused any trouble, and were not feared.

The last known member of the Beathucks, the native Indians of Newfoundland, was Shanadthit (renamed Mary March by the English). She died in 1829. The French appear to have brought Micmac Indians from the continent during the French-English struggle to dominate Newfoundland. But the Micmacs had existed in considerable numbers on the island, perhaps as far back as to have been there at the same time as the Beathucks. At least some were seasonal hunters and trappers of the inland mountains, and one family owned and operated a fishing boat somewhere on the south coast.

Now Andrew and Frank had "taken possession" of the valley with its virgin forest, and the river with salmon, trout, char, and gaspereau. They were ready, then, to capitalize on the situation. They bought a partial interest in the schooner *Bonnie* from John Garson, loaded her with logs for sawing and masts to sell or trade in Nova Scotia, and returned with a load of coal from Sydney for Port aux Basques.

The coastal ferrying was profitable, and from the experienced ship captain with whom they were now associated, they learned the art of sailing oceangoing schooners. But it meant leaving the women and children alone in the remote valley for months at a time. This was not acceptable to the widow Fanny and sealed her decision to take her three daughters and return to Harbor Le Cou. However, before she left, a government official and sport-fisherman, Mr. Squarry from Port aux Basques, there to fish the river, met and advised Fanny to apply for a grant to protect her sons' interest in their pioneered land. Mr. Squarry was a surveyor. His job with the government was to promote and properly record the land grants that had recently been approved following the end of two hundred years of unfriendly violations of treaty fishing rights. After local conflicts, the treaty rights ended in 1904. The remaining French population was forced to leave, and the Newfoundland government began making land grants to the English settlers. Before he left, Mr. Squarry measured the land and took with him the information necessary for a grant application. As a result of his visit, applications were made. After long delays, Frank and Andrew Strickland were awarded three land grants, one dated 1904 and two in 1908. These grants consisted of essentially small "house lots" totaling only an acre or two on the west side of the valley and along the area where the river entered the bay. The village took the name North Bay from the area called that before it was settled.

Thomas Farrell, with his wife Elizabeth (Strickland, from West Point), daughter Annie, and six sons, Reuben, Josiah, Edward, Herbert, Sidney, and Eugene, had become well established since moving to East Bay in 1892. He and the boys built a small house that first summer in which they were crowded but warm during the coming winter. Before the snow came, they also built a deep lean-to against the steep mountain behind the house as shelter for his cow and a dozen sheep. The following summer he built a storehouse in which to keep his boatbuilding tools and fishing equipment; they also lived in it while he built a new house twenty-four feet by sixteen feet using many of the boards and timbers from the old house.

He fished for cod and trapped lobster, marketing his catches at the fish plant back at La Poile. The cow provided milk, butter and

Elizabeth (Strickland) Farrell, wife of Thomas Farrell and daughter Annie.

cheese; the sheep supplied wool for their winter clothing and a welcome change from their usual fish diet. He built rowboats and sold them for one dollar a foot., ten dollars if the keel measured ten feet, fifteen dollars for fifteen feet. He built himself a boat with a twenty-one foot keel, seven feet wide. Two sixteen foot oars allowed two men to row it easily when empty (much harder and slower when loaded). They used it to transport hay for the cow and sheep from the meadows in the valley at North Bay and for the logs needed to build the boats. Sons Reuben and Josiah cut these logs using a pit saw. When Reuben went with John Chatney to Grand Bruit and got a job paying fifteen dollars per month with board and room, younger brother Edward pulled the other end of the pit saw to cut boards and ribs.

To have men in the village and neighbors for their mother and sisters while they were away on the *Bonnie*, Frank and Andrew

Thomas Farrell with sons Edward and Josiah.

convinced Thomas to move his family to North Bay. That his daughter Annie was by then married to Frank and already living at North Bay was further incentive, particularly for Elizabeth, to accept the invitation. Andrew took Thomas's house at East Bay in return for lumber and material at North bay with which to build a house there. Thomas paid the Stricklands seventy-five cents per year as rental for the land. He built away from the river and in back of Andrew's house, only a hundred yards from where a good-sized brook ended its thousand-foot fall from the mountain.

4

The Thomas Farrell Family

At the time of his move from East Bay to North Bay, Thomas Farrell's large family consisted of his wife, six sons, and one daughter. Daughter Annie had recently married Frank Strickland and was already living at North Bay. Thomas's twenty-one-foot boat, powered by the double sweeps in the hands of his young sons, provided the transportation for two dogs, a cow, fourteen hens, two roosters, and a dozen sheep to North Bay when the new house had a roof and walls. There was little else to move: the iron kitchen stove for heat and cooking, the kettles and dishes; hand tools; two axes, a buck saw, a two-man cross-cut saw and sharpening stones for cutting timber and sawing logs; a shovel and an iron bar; nets and line and hooks for fishing; and his lobster pots.

There was little spare time what with the carpentry work needed to finish the inside of the house and providing fish and ptarmigan, caribou, and rabbits to feed the large family; but that spare time was spent building boats. Spruce and fir logs were cut by the riverside and then pulled into and down the river by ropes and current and ashore on the granular rock beach. Pulled again by ropes, the larger logs on rollers, to where the pit saw had been installed, they were sawed into boards. The huge yellow birch was hewn by ax and adze to size and shapes for keels and ribs.

Now it was the fall of 1908. The three houses were situated within fifty yards of one another, each with a small barn for hay, a cow, and sheep. Stumps had been removed where the houses were built, but many nearby remained in various degrees of removal by digging and fire. Evidence of spotty attempts to raise

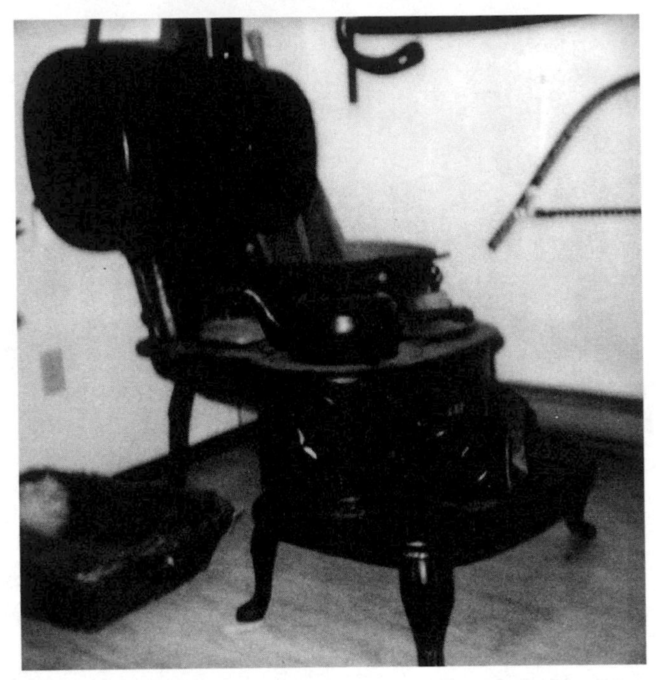

Stove used for cooking and heating. High oven heated by stove pipe. Picture courtesy of Port aux Basque Museum.

a few hills of potatoes, some carrots, and turnips (rutabagas) showed where the Strickland women and children had planted a few seeds the previous spring. Rose and lilac bushes struggled to survive beside the doorways. Dead leaves on three small mounds between the houses showed where the rhubarb would sprout again next spring. On a hillside beyond the village and west of the river a sizable plot had been cleared of grass and alders and then been burned, to reduce competition for the native wild blueberry bushes.

The garden would be women's and children's work, perhaps with some help from the men to remove heavy rocks and roots. For the Farrell men—who included boys big enough to run errands or drag brush—cutting and dragging in the firewood, cutting it to stove length with an ax, piling the brush close around the house to keep the winter wind and snow from penetrating, were added to the routine seasonal work of providing food for the family and hay for the livestock. And each dug a deep trench, six feet wide, into the side of the bank by the small stream that reached the bay at the river mouth. They lined it with logs on the back and both sides. They added a sturdy log roof that they insulated and shingled, and a substantial door at the front. It would be their refrigerator in summer, freeze-proof storage in winter. And there may have been times when the men rowed back from Rose Blanche, or from cutting logs upriver, only to be told that unless they wanted salted cod or salted caribou for supper, they would have to go out and catch a fish or snare an arctic hare.

Insofar as possible, basic food was obtained from the sea, the river, and the mountain valleys. But the ships they built and the sons they raised sailed to near and far places and returned with staples from Canada, the United States, the Caribbean Islands, and across the Atlantic. They brought flour and sugar in barrels of 196 and 300 pounds respectively, rice and oatmeal, molasses in a tierce of fifty gallons, rum in kegs, tea, beans, barrels of salted pork and beef, and potatoes. They also brought the hardware for their boats, cotton cloth for their clothes, and leather and shoes for their feet.

Though they were able to raise only a few potatoes, cabbage, and rutabaga, the coastal freighters provided good service from Prince Edward Island, where these vegetables were plentiful.

A typical breakfast consisted of tea, toast, eggs, oatmeal with milk and molasses or hard bread soaked in milk, and pancakes with molasses or sugar syrup.

Dinner at noon might include potatoes, caribou or mutton (fresh, salted, or canned), with carrots, rutabaga, and onions. The meat might be replaced by fowl, duck, or ptarmigan, or by fish—salmon, trout, cod seasonally fresh; otherwise canned or salted and dried—with rice. There were dry beans for baking or stewing. They made soups, stews, and chowders. They roasted and fried on their low woodstoves fired by hot-burning alder or chips from the boatyard. And the hungry men were ready for a repeat full supper after logging upriver or working on the boats until dark.

Vegetable "cellars" dug into bank of Drinking Brook.

The village was established. The three homes were those of Andrew Strickland, his wife, Martha, and two small children; Frank Strickland, with his wife, Annie; and Thomas Farrell, with wife Elizabeth and sons Josiah, Edward, Herbert, Sidney, and Eugene. The Farrell boys were already growing into manhood; Josiah was ready to take over family leadership. To cook and wash the clothes for such a family—having to carry the water in wooden buckets from the stream, wash the clothing on the rock shore, and hang them to dry on outside lines between the trees—would seem to be more than one woman could accomplish. The younger boys carried much of the water from Drinking Brook (a second nearby brook on the other side of the village was lined with outhouses) and brought in the wood. They also occasionally provided trout or salmon or rabbit for meals. But the cow had to be milked, the milk "set," the cream skimmed off and churned into butter, wool sheared from their dozen sheep and then cleaned, carded, spun into yarn, and knitted or woven into material for usable winter clothes for all. There were noses to blow and diapers to change and babies to bathe; floors to sweep and wash; berries that the children had picked to can in glass jars or to make jelly or jam; bread to mix and raise and bake. And with anyone very sick or badly hurt having to travel sixty miles to the nearest doctor, "mother" brewed and dispensed the medicine, cleaned, disinfected, and bandaged the cuts and bruises, and splinted the broken fingers. She was also the schoolteacher, teaching her children to read and write and figure. (There would be no schoolhouse at North Bay for another twelve years.)

Frank's wife, Annie, helped. She had escaped the baby-sitting for her six younger brothers when she married Frank; but now Andrew and Martha's young family needed attention; and soon Annie would start her own family...

Thomas continued the seasonal cod fishing and lobster trapping; but as his sons grew older and took an active part in the work, he progressed from building rowboats to sell for a dollar a foot to building a skiff each year of thirty-five-foot length with forty-foot masts and sold them without rigging for $180 apiece. Josiah and his younger brother Edward (Ned) were sawing the boards with the pit saw and taking an active part in the logging and boat construction. After having helped his father and younger brothers build four of the skiffs, Josiah thought that his father should be getting a higher price for his work (and no doubt Josiah himself wanted more pay). He reached an agreement with his father whereby he would take the latest-built skiff to sell and keep any amount over the $180 that he would pay his father. He then purchased the material, fitted it out, and was able to sell it for $330, making a profit of seventy-five dollars for himself. Up until this time, Thomas and the boys had always worked together.

Joe and Ned then built their first model for a skiff. A boatbuilder from Harbor Le Cou visited North Bay. He used models to build boats and examined the one Joe and Ned had constructed. "I believe she will sail," was his judgment. The boys built a skiff from the model, and it proved to be a good boat: They sold it for $400.

Encouraged and confident with this success, they decided to build a small schooner sixty feet long and sixteen feet wide that would need ten feet of water when in ballast to float.

It was winter. They convinced a young friend who was visiting from West Point to accompany them up the river to cut spruce and fir logs for the forty-eight-foot masts, the forty-foot boom, and the inner planking, as well as silver birch for the keel, ribs, and outer planking. Three miles upriver, where it was convenient to find the trees close to the still unfrozen water, they worked for five days. They cut eleven selected logs that they pushed and pulled into the river to begin the voyage down to the village. The friend, upon returning, was asked about the trip: He would never go back again, he said, "It was worse than war, where one occasionally had time to light his pipe, for which there was no time up the river."

By spring, the masts and boom had been scraped clean of bark, the logs were sawed, the keel laid. They spent a good part of the summer building the hull of the schooner. When it was finished they had not sold it. Frank and Andrew Strickland had condemned the *Bonnie* that summer. She had a new mainsail and jumbo jib and Joe and Ned bought her for the rigging. Mr. Le Sellieur at the store in La Poile had a foresail and some blocks. They towed the hull to West Point and fitted her out. Without a buyer by the first of August, they sailed her to Rose Blanche to have her measured, then to Channel, where they had to wait eight days to get papers.

With the condemning of the *Bonnie*, Frank and Andrew returned to North Bay to build boats. Joe and Ned were then free to be away. They hired a licensed ship captain and sailed their schooner with a load of logs to Sydney, Nova Scotia. The ship was strongly tested in a fierce storm en route and the skipper told them it handled well and was seaworthy. They delivered the logs and loaded coal for Port aux Basques. Still with no buyer, they made a second trip, this one starting in company with Charlie Clark's fifty-ton schooner from Rose Blanche and joined by a one hundred-ton foreign-built vessel belonging to R. Moulton, a merchant from Grand Bruit. They kept pace with the smaller ship but could not keep up with the larger one when she put up extra sail. When they left Sydney for the return trip, they were accompanied by a schooner of similar size as theirs and skimmed past her to hold a long lead. When they arrived at Petites, a man there offered $1100, and they sold their schooner. After all expenses were paid, they had little profit; but they had learned a great deal and established a reputation for boat-building that stood them in good stead for many years.

5

Building Boats

Both John Strickland and Thomas Farrell built their own boats—at least the rowboats necessary for any transportation beyond their own villages, the skiffs with which to transport logs or a cow or whatever else needed to be taken to another location along the coast, and the fishing boats with which they earned much of their cash or barter income. Just as the knowledge and ability required of their craft had been passed on to them by their fathers, they too passed it on to their sons.

Andrew and Frank Strickland had a turn at "coasting" with the *Bonnie*. Josiah and Edward had their turn at sea with two trips to Nova Scotia on the schooner they had built. Then married and with children, living at the mouth of the river valley filled with a virgin forest and at the head of a navigable bay, they were ready to remain home to build boats according to the specifications of various buyers.

Most of the trees—yellow birch, spruce, and fir—were cut during the long winters. Some were hand dragged by rope down to the village on the river ice, others were left to be floated down on the high water of spring. Some were sawed by pit saw near where they had grown, the six-foot-high rugged platform built on a suitable spot, and the sawn planks, with one end on a bobsled, then dragged by men with ropes to the village.

Ernest Farrell, grandson of Thomas and son of Edward, describes the process of building a boat on an out-of-door platform, summer or winter:

> First would be the keel. It would be joined from two pieces to make it the desired length, usually made from

Logs brought down river.

birch, as it would be a long while in salt water. The keel would be five inches thick and eight or nine inches wide, then a two-inch shoe or strip would be nailed to the bottom of the keel to help make the joint stronger. Where the keel was joined together it would be held in place with half-inch or five-eighths galvanized bolts and tightened together with a washer and a nut, all galvanized.

Once the keel was made up to the desired length, the headpiece, or stem as it was called, would then be attached, both stem and keel laying on one side. Once it was all lined fair with each other and cut to make a strong joint, the stem would be attached to the end of the keel in the same manner and held with bolts, washers, and nuts. Once complete, it would then be righted up and set in place, put plumb and lined up with the keel, then braced in place to hold it there. Then the work would begin with the back end, building up the back and putting it in line with the rest of the work. All these parts at the back were fastened down in place with three-quarter-inch galvanized iron to preferred length; and everything was set in line with each other. All these sections were of birch or witch-hazel (some call it white birch), a

North Bay village in winter.

harder wood than the yellow birch when it got good and dry. All the wood material was cut and dried in the sun before it was used; and they always tried to keep a certain amount on hand so to have dry timber to work with. The large-size boats were ribbed with four-inch by four-inch timber, cut with different crooks in it, some with a little bend and more with a lot of bend. For any crooked shape it was marked off with a mold as near to the right shape as possible and then sawed out with a rip saw.

When they first began to build, all the framing to build a boat was hewn out with an ax; and it was a slow and tiring job. Once a section of the frame was all hewn out, it was placed on the markings that were made on the floor and held in place, then more pieces were laid over the joints and all held in place with wooden trunnels, as they were called (much the same as a dowel). The holes were drilled through both pieces of timber one and one-eighth in size, and the wooden trunnels were driven in tight to hold it secure. All of the boats were built from models which they made themselves and would be shown to the person who would want the boat to see if it was satisfactory for him. It was all taken off on a one-inch scale.

The only boats that had a bent frame would be a small boat such as a rowboat or a fishing boat of up to twenty feet

Boat just out of shop being moved to river.

or so in length. Ribs for the larger boats were sawed to shape. Models were made for any boat, of the desired length, and marked off at certain spaces. A mold would then be made and set in its proper place, then battens nailed along the length around eight or ten inches apart. After all was secure, they would then bend the timbers (planking boards) all through the boat.

Bending would be required of timber of any special shape such as at the bottom of the boat. Some planking would need quite a twist as well as a bend. Also the framing for small boats of a size of one inch by two- or three-quarter inch and by one and one-half inch. We had a box about fourteen to eighteen feet long made as snug as possible. It would be set up on a frame, then a forty-five-gallon metal barrel placed under the box and connected with a two-inch pipe. The barrel, filled with water with a fire built beneath, when boiling, would steam planks in the box, making them soft enough to bend and twist.

Ernest Farrell also described the tools used to build the boats before any kind of power was available: The sawmill, when water was available, saved considerable time and work when sawing logs, but it was of no help in "chopping" out the four-inch-thick curved ribs of a boat or shaping the bow extension of the keel; and the chopping procedure with ax and adze was not to Josiah's liking.

> The timber [log] was ripped into boards by a pit saw. One man would be at the top and another would be underneath. Where my father and uncle had their place to rip timber was at the place next to the mill that I later had. They built a place there for working out of the weather. The flooring was about six feet above the ground, giving space for a man below. An opening was in the floor (longer than the log to be sawed) to set the timber onto to cut into boards. Boards were laid along each side of the timber to stand onto and the timber held in place by dogs. These were called "set dogs." It was a slow process; but this was the way they worked. To build the house to work in, they took their saw into the brush [forest] and built the frame to saw their timber. This was done out of doors in all seasons for several years before they built a workshop.
>
> The framing for the boats was hewn on the two sides with an ax. Then once the sides were hewn down to make the timber the thickness that was needed, it was then laid down and marked off to any shape that they needed and at any angle. There were always plenty of chips to take home to burn. I quite often would be taking them to our home. Day after day they would be working on those jobs until the frame was complete.
>
> The cross-cut saw was used quite often, a man at each end to cut off anything that was a little heavy to cut with a hand saw, which was used very often for cut-off work. The planking was sawn with the bark on both edges to be cut any shape needed. It would then be marked off, lined to the desired shape, then placed on two sawhorses. The edges were ripped off with a hand saw, then set at the workbench

Launched hull in river.

and dressed down, giving it the angle at the edges so that it would have a little opening outside to make it easier to lay the caulking into. It was caulked in with oakum. Both sides and deck would have that done.

For drilling holes in the planking and decking or any other holes that were needed to fasten material together, a hand brace was used. Each workman had two or three of these. Any hole that was needed would be done with a brace bit. The largest would be three-quarters of an inch, down to one-eighth of an inch. When planking, two brace bits were used, one with the drill for any size nail, another for what was called a countersink to let the head of the nail sink into the wood so it could be filled. After the boat was completely planked and nails set in, it then had to be planed down again to take off any edges that would stand out a bit from the other and to give it smoothing. It would take about a day to get the edges all level with each other. For doing this work one used a fourteen-inch plane. To straighten edges of things that needed to be straight, an eighteen-inch plane was used. When one had to level the edges of the planking in the hollow of the bottom of the boat, a smaller tool was

Rigged boat being towed out by buyer.

used. It was called a boat scraper. It was about three inches wide with a two-inch blade attached to a handle so it could bend any way.

When our parents were at these jobs, all lumber for these boats was dressed by a hand plane. The decking was dressed both sides as well as the edges, also giving a little opening to caulk between the boards. The deck boards were four inches wide and one and one-half inches thick dressed to cover the top and to put a small house-like on the front to get down where they would eat and sleep. The inside would be done all with boards one and one-eighth inches thick. It took many a day to dress it all up and was very tiring. Many a day I worked on this.

The preferred name for boats twenty tons or a little over built at North Bay was skiffs, above that and over thirty tons were called small schooners. The designations of jack boats or western fishing boats were not used at North Bay.

The skiffs, as we called them, had two masts and sails (and later motors) and measured from thirty-five to about sixty feet in length. When sails were the only power, and no wind blowing to get into or out of a harbor, the crew would get in a dory, attach a line, and tow it by rowing, a slow process. With the availability of motors, it was some time before it was learned how to build to install the motor and propeller.

Upon completion, each boat was measured, length and width, by a representative of the Department of Fisheries and the tonnage capacity computed. The department would then advance payment in an amount based on the tonnage to the purchaser (subsidized) to help cover the cost. Roughly figured, a skiff of thirty-five feet in length would have a ten-or twelve-ton capacity. The buyer would prefer a particular size depending upon the size of the crew to do the fishing, some using a three-man crew, others five or more for the larger schooners.

6

To Waterpower and Oxen

In 1909, Andrew Strickland was, at age 33, the "old man" of the younger generation of the village. He had married Martha Taylor, the daughter of John Taylor, of Northwest Cove, and was ready to settle down and raise his family. He and brother Frank built and sold six more two-masted skiffs during the next three years.

Following the sale of their boat, Josiah and Edward along with father, built and sold another and then another. With a good reputation established, they continued building boats. At age twenty, Joe was ready to "go in for himself." Ned at age eighteen was ready to go with him, and they started working on their own.

The imaginative and aggressive Josiah had taken over the family leadership. He married Julia Stone, of West Point, and built a big house on a grant of land a hundred yards or so east of his father's home. Edward married Annie Anderson, also from West Point, and built on a grant across Drinking Brook near where the boats were launched. During the next eighteen years the brothers built and sold forty-six nonrigged hulls that were launched at North Bay.

There would be no further immigration to North Bay until the Taylor family arrived seventeen years later. The available labor during those years for the men who financed and took the risks to build the boats were the men themselves and their families. In 1909, they consisted of Andrew Strickland (thirty-three), his son Frederick (nine), Frank Strickland (thirty-one), Thomas Farrell (fifty), and his sons, Josiah (twenty-six), Edward (twenty-three), Sidney (seventeen), Eugene (fifteen), William (thirteen), and Her-

North Bay village with government financed school.

bert (eleven). It is probable that they hired George Taylor from Northwest Harbor and Alex Strickland from East Bay when they needed extra help.

The difficult, slow, and monotonous job of sawing logs with a pit saw had always been a time-limiting factor in the building of boats at North Bay. Josiah Farrell, in his "coasting" days had seen, or at least heard of, water-powered sawmills. In about 1914 he and Edward first sketched on paper a sluice leading to a huge overrun waterwheel with the necessary axles, shafts, and pulleys to turn a saw. They then went in back of the houses about one hundred yards to where the small brook landed among the rocks after its wild flight down the steep mountainside. The brothers built a sluice two feet wide and six inches deep that extended four hundred and twenty feet down through the rough area and at the lower end parallel to and just below the bank with the row of vegetable cellars. There they built the huge waterwheel, twelve feet in diameter and eighteen inches wide, with deep cups to hold the water, its weight to turn the wheel. The four-inch iron axle (and surrounding wooden pulley wheels) twisted off before

Sluice of Drinking Brook to saw mill.

they had used it very much. They replaced it with a larger one, which held.

It took time and trials before the right axle and pulley sizes proved workable, but eventually the forty-inch circular saw they had purchased at Le Sellieur's store in La Poile was sawing logs.

They constructed a substantial building over the site to protect the equipment, to handle the logs, and to store the boards and planks. The logs were dragged into the building by ropes on rollers, then lifted onto the saw table, all by hand.

Now, after more than a dozen years of building boats outside in all extremes of weather, Josiah and Edward built a huge "workshop" over the area between the sawmill building and the river where boats had always been built. Though not heated, it offered protection from the wind and avoided the necessity of shoveling snow from the partially built frames before starting the day's work. It was a high building, twenty feet or more from the ridgepole of the low-pitched roof, sixty-nine feet long and twenty-three feet wide, with plenty of room inside to work on a sixty-foot hull.

When trees near the river for miles up the valley had all been cut, it became a long drag by manpower with ropes to get the logs to the river. Soon after Josiah and Edward had the water-powered sawmill in working order, Frank purchased an ox and

Ox hauling logs to mill.

brought it from La Poile to North Bay in his boat. He had a problem harnessing the ox until a visiting minister, the Reverend Seeley, suggested he try a horse collar. With some adjustments, this worked well. Edward Farrell had a bull at the time. Using a horse collar on the beast, he put the bull to work as well.

It was no mistake that Edward had a bull. With cow ownership averaging one to a family, it was necessary to have a bull available to get the cows bred. The usual system was for members of the village to purchase through Le Sellieur's store at La Poile each spring several bred cows and a young bull capable of service. The bull and any infertile or poor milking cows would be butchered in the fall when the weather was cold enough to keep meat frozen. It saved hand-scythed hay needed during the winter for the milking cows, the oxen, and the sheep. When a family animal was butchered any surplus meat not needed by the other villagers would be taken to La Poile or Rose Blanche and sold.

Andrew built a small bobsled on which one end of a large log or of several smaller logs could be bound and dragged behind the ox to the river or to the village. Soon several family members had each purchased an ox and built a small barn down near the workshop and sawmill.

7

Working Days

The sawmill, when water was available, saved considerable time and work when sawing logs, but it was of no help in "chopping" out the four-inch thick curved ribs of a boat or shaping the bow extension of the keel; and the chopping procedure with ax and adze was not to Josiah's liking.

It was time again to "invent" improvements in production. Josiah made sketches of a band saw big enough to handle large timbers. He ordered nine saws, three each of different widths, half inch, one inch, and one and a half inches, from the Canada Saw Company. He built two "wheels" (pulleys) and set up a series of shafts and pulleys in the sawmill. When the saws came, he got the machine to operating. All nine saws broke before he had sawed out a single rib. He wrote to Canada Saw, and was advised that his pulleys were too small and the saw too thick. They suggested the proper measurements. They also wrote that the band saw was to be pulled down through the log, not up through, as they were doing. Josiah then changed the drive from the lower to the top shaft, as was suggested.

His new "wheels" were three feet in diameter, the band saw, fourteen feet eight inches in circumference. He bought four, and though one occasionally broke, he was able to braise it and continue using it. His imagination and ingenuity once again reduced the labor requirement and speeded up the building of boats.

Sawing with waterpower, again like the salmon and cod fishing and the logging and guiding for caribou or moose, was seasonal. For a while in spring, when the snow was melting on the high tableland, there was a fairly even flow of water; but when nights

Jack and Arthur Farrell returning from logging up river.

were cold enough to stop the snowmelt on the mountains, there was no power until the morning sun had again started the melt. Without a sizable and adjustable water storage area, and after the annual spring snowmelt, enough to turn the water wheel depended on when it rained. In dry years, they still reverted to the pit saw when the spring-sawed board supply had dwindled.

Snow came early and deep to the La Poile River valley, and marked the season for cutting trees and getting them down the river and ready to be sawed. From three to five men with the help of several teenaged boys would go upriver with axes and cross-cut saws, cut the trees near the river, and ready them to be floated to the village during high water. They would stay for four or five days, bringing along home-cooked meals suitable for warming over an outside fire. Each family had at least one sturdy dog that was trained to haul homemade sleds in which food and tools were transported to the workplace. When they returned, another party would go up for a period of cutting and dragging for four to five days. They built a small lean-to near where they cut the trees, using it mostly for sleeping because they worked from dawn until dark, or for times when they were caught upriver in a bad storm.

The oxen increased the need to cut more hay than was being used by the family cows and sheep. The men built crude sheds at the edge of the trees near the island meadows where the native hay grew and stored it there to winter feed the oxen when logging nearby.

The men who stayed back in the village spent their time pulling the pit saws and hewing the keels and ribs and building boats. There was meat to procure to feed their families, much of which came as ptarmigan and Arctic hares to supplement the salted, smoked, and canned meat and fish. Thus they could avoid butchering a sheep or lamb or a rare steer from their small livestock supply.

In spring the high and roaring river delivered any logs that had not been dragged over the ice by hand or oxen during the winter. The men rescued them from the river current and the sea, towed them to the beach where the small stream entered the river, and pulled them onto shore to safe storage until they could get them sawed. They long remembered one year when high water, an ice jam, and a fierce storm carried their winter cutting of logs to sea, all lost. With the spring rains, and the breakup of river ice making it impossible to get up or near the river, all hands turned to sawing logs and to building boats.

It was July before the lilacs bloomed by their front doors and the salmon run was in full swing. What a welcome change of diet from the canned or salted cod and caribou when fresh salmon could be placed on the dinner table! Though the run varied in both numbers and size of fish, there were few years when they caught none. Some of the salmon were salted, smoked, and dried and then hung in attic rooms.

Then the bay filled with cod on their annual migration. They were netted and jigged. Some were rowed to La Poile and sold or bartered. They were split, entrails and the backbone removed, and salted and laid out on flakes to dry. They were fried and boiled and made into chowder. Other fish were known as salmon and trout; but cod was THE FISH, and it dominated the daily work, the meals, and the conversations whenever and wherever two or more people met. Though hard work, it was also exciting, particularly for the young boys when they were first allowed to go with the men to the nets and to jig. Briefly, at least, even chores could be neglected, perhaps carrying the wooden buckets of water from the Drinking Brook and digging to make a garden. The endless errands were left for sisters and mothers as the boys learned where and how to set the nets and where to jig while waiting to pull the nets. They watched the eagles and osprey drop from the sky to snatch an unwary fish from too near the top of the water, watched the porpoise and an occasional whale in the wide part of the bay where it divided into North and East.

But the fishing ended. It would be another month before the sea trout swarmed in the tidewater at the mouth of the river, waiting for their time to return to their own beginnings. A few salmon straggled up the river during the length of summer; but now it was time to build boats again. The hammers pounded, the saws scratched, and the shavings rolled from the hand planes as men fitted ribs to keels and boards to ribs and planks to decks and their ships took shape.

8

Special Days

A launching, unlike Christmas, New Year's, weddings, and birthdays, was no occasion for a party. First the up-to-sixty-foot hull had to be moved from where it was built to where a high tide could float it. That could be fifty yards or more, so every able-bodied man in the village turned his attention and physical efforts to the job at hand. Specially built log rollers were put in place. Rope-and-block pulleys were attached and anchored. Inch by inch, the hull was moved down the incline and toward a rendezvous with its connection to the oceans of the world. It was slow progress, the tackle ropes pulled by brute human strength.

As the hull progressed down the natural "slip," rollers were moved from those behind and passed to ahead of the boat and the tightened ropes and blocks reset. Patience and muscles cooperated under the direction of the more experienced men and the process went forward in an orderly manner until the hulls reached the point at which the high tide would float them. A launching was just another day's work at North Bay.

With masts and booms and finishing still to be done, the boatbuilders would be working on it for some time before the skiff was ready to deliver to the buyer.

Parties were reserved for weddings, birthdays, and holidays. Then berry pies were baked and cakes were frosted. Most of the men, even the young and single ones, were too bashful to participate in the dancing when the accordion music began (and, in later years, when the "wind each side" of the record played on the phonograph); but they joined enthusiastically in the singing of mostly hymns. News of the occasion and party would have

Boat ready to be launched.

spread down the bay and to villages along the coast, and friends and relatives came in small boats and skiffs to join the festivities. Guns fired salutes at wedding receptions, the men using powder only in reloaded shells. Summer Sundays, if the weather was fair, were also visiting days, when families got together, often sharing picnic lunches. Or a group might go to one of the great marshes to pick marsh berries, partridgeberries, bake apple; or to the grassland meadows on the river islands for wild strawberries; or to a rocky barren for blueberries. What berries were not eaten fresh, the women preserved in glass jars to make pies and puddings from them during the winter months.

Caribou and moose meat, as well as salmon, was also preserved in glass jars and stored in the side hill vegetable cellars for winter consumption. The number of caribou that came in late season to feed on the valley islands was unpredictable. Weather conditions affected their food supply both on the high barrens and in the valley. One year Edward, while hunting to fill his own larder, came upon a herd and was able to kill several of the large males within a mile of the village. He poled his boat from the village upstream to a spot not distant from the dressed animals and enlisted his younger brother's help to drag and load them. Then they rowed the boat, weighted down with surplus carcasses, the nine miles to La Poile to sell the meat. Either the herd had passed close enough to La Poile that villagers there had obtained their own supply or the offered price was not satisfactory; but Edward and his brother rowed on to Rose Blanche, some twenty-seven miles beyond, and sold the caribou for ten cents a pound. The animals averaged three hundred pounds apiece—amounting to a considerable addition to their sparse cash income.

That nine miles plus the twenty-seven to Rose Blanche and another twenty-seven miles to Port aux Basques was the same distance to the nearest doctor. And the only transportation was a rowboat, sometimes with a small sail if the wind was right, or, if in a rough sea, to steady the boat. The need for a doctor—and the need to know if one was needed—was the greatest worry of each mature individual in the village.

With a considerable number of children now in the village, the boatbuilders applied to the government of Newfoundland for money to build and operate a school. Time and again, the request was ignored or denied. In 1914 they held their first annual party to raise money to build and support their school, which would also be used as a church. It had one room with a woodstove but without running water or toilet facilities. Some of the early teachers were Mabel Courtney, Stella Maugar, Earl Neil, Alan Parsons, Ellen Billard, and Harold Milbourne. They had slates and pencils and painted blackboards and chalk, but it would be another ten years before the government built a larger schoolhouse and provided books. The first, according to Max Strickland, who attended the school, was the Royal Reader.

One of the more pleasant seasonal jobs came in late July or early August, when the thick blackflies were no longer around, the weather usually comfortable, the days longer, and salmon still in pools, and the sea-run trout beginning their run up the river. This job was to cut the hay and get it stored in the several small storage sheds built to keep it for the oxen when they were pulling logs the next winter. Enough hay was brought back to the village to feed the cows and sheep.

The native hay grew thick on the meadow islands, often called the flats, between the two branches of the river. It was cut by men swinging scythes. One cut a swath five or six feet wide, and another and then another man followed, each leaving long windrows of hay that would be shaken out to dry in the sun. Once dry, the men used a large hay rake with twelve-inch wooden teeth to gather the hay into ricks. They used pitchforks to carry it to the sheds, where it was trod down to get the maximum amount into the available space.

They built a two-wheeled hay cart with shaves to fit an ox. The ox was harnessed with a horse collar and suitable fittings. There was no blacksmith at North Bay. Iron used in boatbuilding was ordered by measurement as needed from a supplier in Port aux Basques, as were the ox shoes. The wheels for their hay carts were made of wood. Iron for the rims, two and a half inches wide, was ordered in ten-foot lengths. Until the breast brace was invented, the men used a hand brace to drill holes about ten inches apart for nails to fasten the rim as it was bent around the wheel. Axles for hay wagons were also ordered from Port aux Basques, one and a half inches square and three feet long, with end sections turned for bearings. The axle turned with the wheel, each axle and wheel on its separate wood bearings.

There might still be wild strawberries for the children to pick. Family members would bring picnic dinners from the village for the working men, and lunch might include fresh trout cooked in a skillet over an open fire on the rocks close to the cold running water. The women and children might remove shoes and socks to paddle in a backwater, sun-warmed pool, or pick daisies, blue iris, and asters.

Ernest Farrell described the hay carts.

> About the two wheel carts that I mentioned in my letter. I will try to draw and explain the shape as near as I can, it may also be a bit difficult for you to get the right idea.
>
> On the oxen's back, a small saddle was made to fit their

back to help carry the load. About this shape as I will try to draw for you.

A groove was cut over the top such as for the pole to go into, the pole was attached to the tongues at one side, passed in the groove, then tied to the other side. Also it had hitches to keep the load steady.

This is where they hitched to the end of the tongue. The oxen wore yokes to haul with over their necks and were attached to the end of the tongues.

The bottom has boards spaced a short distance apart. Also the sides and front end. The bottom about five feet wide with sides slanted out a little, length of the loading space around nine or ten feet, sides around three feet or so high. The back end would be laced across the opening. After loading it would be all tied down, due to rough riding over the stones.

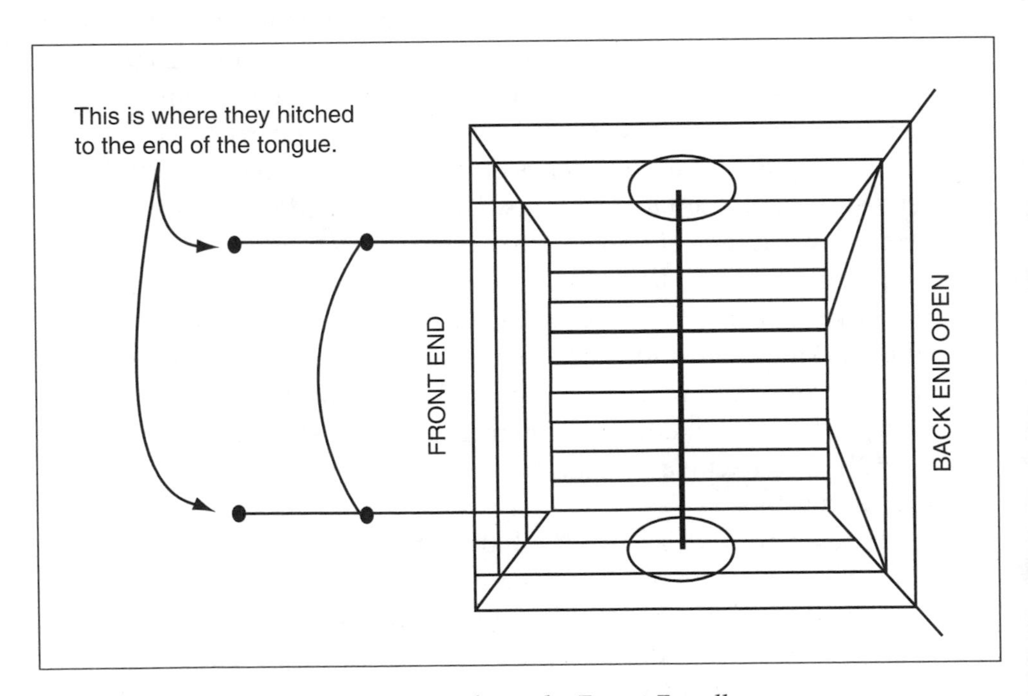

Diagram of ox-pulled hay wagon drawn by Ernest Farrell.

9

Individuals of North Bay

The men of North Bay were of average stature or shorter, five feet seven or eight inches in height. Andrew was a little chubby, weighing about 170 pounds. He was jovial and trusting and friendly to all except anyone who did not treat him fairly. Frank was somewhat heavier. He weighted over 200 pounds, and had broader shoulders and a barrel chest. He particularly liked hunting and fishing. Josiah was thin and wiry—he never weighed more than 140. A hardworking man who never stopped, he said as he grew older, "Only as old as you think you is." He was always smiling and agreeable. His youngest son, Jack, remembered him as "a man among men, a genius, very religious, good natured, and he did the work of five men." Each of these men sported mustaches of different designs until shaving clean in later life.

Jack recalled the first year he worked building boats with his father. During the summer he had access to his father's boat with outboard motor and made frequent trips evenings and weekends from North Bay to La Poile and other coastal villages to be "where the action was." He charged the gas for the motor in La Poile when making trips to town for his father to pick up supplies. That fall, when the bay ice ended the pleasure trips, there came a payday when Josiah laid down the list of fuel charges alongside Jack's work time record and asked how much he wanted to apply to the account. It took Jack most of the winter to pay the money and he never repeated his charging ways.

The women were, at least as they matured and had their large families, of heavier build, perhaps in part due to being well muscled from the physical work that was their lot. While some had lighter hair than others, it seems there were no blond women at North Bay.

Each of the women of North Bay was a "medicine woman" to a degree, taking care of the minor cuts and bruises of men and children,—"I cut my finger," "I bruised my knee." But there were also the babies to be "midwifed."

Expectant women usually requested Lillian Riles, from the coast, who had midwifed more than three hundred births. At the estimated date of birth, she would come and stay with the family until the baby arrived and remain until all was well. But when she had conflicts of appointments, or was late to arrive, there were other competent midwives available, among them Emma Francis and Priscilla Francis. Julia Stone Farrell, wife of Josiah, was usually present at each birth and fully capable of handling the situation if Lillian Riles did not get there. Her sister, Esther (Essie) Strickland, had come to North Bay with her daughters Violet and Hilda to keep house for George Taylor Jr. His wife had died in twin childbirth two years earlier. Esther was an experienced midwife. She was twice midwife for daughter Violet and once for daughter Hilda. In fact, midwifery seemed to be a family talent. Violet also midwifed, including one of her own births: She had decided to go to the hospital in Burgeo to have her third baby, but when she arrived, all the hospital beds were filled. The doctor came to a relative's home where Violet was staying and examined her. The baby would not arrive for several hours, he said, so he would make another house call and return in about two hours. The baby Joan made her appearance fifteen minutes after the doctor left. Violet's relative was fully unprepared, unqualified, and unwilling to participate. Violet became her own midwife, and cut and tied the umbilical cord. A neighbor washed the baby before the doctor returned.

10

Up River

The work of the North Bay boatbuilders started with cutting the trees and was for the most part accomplished during the winter months. Other than that season's difficulties involved with pounding nails, pushing a hand plane, and caulking with oakum, often out of doors or in an unheated building in sub-zero weather, only logs cut when the sap had drained would float in the river. There were also the summer disadvantages of hordes of blackflies and mosquitoes and the sap of spruce and fir that stuck to axes and saws, to hands and clothing.

In 1928, tall and rugged at age fifteen, Ernest Farrell started working with the men. He wielded an ax and pulled one end of a crosscut saw to harvest timber in the high valleys above where the river split, ten or more miles from the village. He vividly remembers winter storms encountered during those years:

> At times we encountered bad weather while working in the bush. It could come up suddenly. Several times as we were traveling over the country (it was shorter from North Bay to go over the barren mountain to the valley where they were working, easier to pull their supply sleds on the tundra snow than through the woods) going to or coming from the logging camp upriver one could not travel on the river ice. A ways beyond Salmon Hole the river branches. One branch goes in an easterly direction, the other in a northerly direction. The one that goes northerly was named Bunker Hill Branch as it traveled around a mountain called Bunker Hill. Sorry I cannot explain how it got that name. At times we would get caught in a snowstorm while coming home or going to the camp.

At one time, five of us were coming home over the country after being in the bush for around two weeks. We had to come home to pick up more provisions, often coming out on a Saturday and returning the following Monday morning if the weather permitted. We got about three quarters of the way over the country (barren mountain top). A bad storm came up. We had a little meat (legal or poached) on our sleighs. The snow was so bad we could not see where we were going. We had to leave our sleighs on the country and try to find our way out. My brother-in-law, James Strickland, had a small dog named Tony with him. As we left the sleighs to pick our way home, the dog stayed with the sleighs. When the weather cleared, we went back to get our sleighs. Tony was lying there on the things that were on the sleigh.

Another time, Max Strickland, Percy Taylor, and I were up in the branch of river that went in the easterly direction. It was called Billard's Brook, named after the people at Grand Bruit with that name who used to trap around that river in the fall. They had a couple of small camps at places along their trapline. In later years we went up that river to cut timber. The three of us had cotton camps set up quite a distance up the river. The river had opened up due to rain and we had to travel over the country to get to the camps. We had brought our supplies across the country to the edge of the tree line, left the sleds there, and packed the supplies on our backs the rest of the way down the mountain to the camps. After being in the bush for two weeks, we decided on this Saturday morning to go back home. We backpacked our few belongings to the sleighs at the edge of the country, loaded the sleighs, hitched our dogs to the sleighs, and headed for home.

After being a little more than halfway home, we looked back over the country to see what appeared to be a heavy snow falling. We had not gone more than another quarter mile before it hit us. There was a strong wind with the snow and it was very cold. It became so thick that we could not see each other. We put on heavier clothes and face masks from our packs and started out again. We soon became separated. I traveled in the direction that I believed to be the right way until I hit a stream that I knew and had to cross on my way out; but it was not at our usual crossing place and I began to move downstream, paying careful attention to what I saw when the snow lightened briefly so that I could see at all. At last I came to the place we usually crossed over.

Max and Percy were not there. It was too cold to stand around for very long, so I kept moving in which I thought was the right way, stopping each time the snow lightened for a minute to try to recognize a familiar mark. At last I came to the cabin that the prospectors had used at the edge of the hill. I waited there for a while but Max and Percy did not arrive, so I went on down the hill to the houses at the village. I went to George Taylor's house to warm up. Max and Percy had not turned up.

I was near finished with my dinner when they dropped in to see if I had been around. They had become lost and went way off track. They were lucky that after a while during one of the breaks from the wind-blown snow they caught sight of something they knew and were able to correct direction and get to the village.

Those severe winter blizzards were no less hazardous to transportation on water than they were on land. Ernest recalled: "Another time James Strickland and I went in a rowboat in early winter to La Poile to pick up a few things. We got to about the entrance to North Bay (from where East Bay separates) coming home and a strong wind came up. We tried several times to get around a small point of land but were blown back each time. At last we put the boat up from the water on the cliff a way. We put most of our things in pack sacks for each and began to climb the mountainside, intending to come in over the country. We got partway up, then the wind all went away as suddenly as it had come. We came back down, put the boat back in the water, and continued rowing on our way. It was dark before we got to the edge of the bay ice. We were good and tired before we got home."

11

Village Review

The winter work of getting logs to the boatyard was speeded up considerably with the use of the ox. Now, when the river was frozen, it became an ice-paved open area down which the logs could be hauled by putting the bobsled under the front ends. With the full village complement of oxen—and an occasional bull or steer—the annual winter logging endeavors rose from five hundred logs to one thousand; and one year they brought down a total of fifteen hundred.

Cash was hard to come by, so whenever an opportunity arose to earn outside income, it was usually taken. Experienced boatbuilders were probably the best all-round carpenters. One summer Josiah and Edward remodeled a two-story house in La Poile and repaired a church in Rose Blanche. Another summer they helped others along the coast, including John Anderson at West Point. With the aid of Mr. Anderson and his sons, they started Monday morning and had the rails on a skiff by Saturday night. Mr. Scotty, a boatbuilder at Channel, couldn't believe it. Their reply was that they did not need him to finish it. A fish merchant, John Moulton, at Burgeo, thinking he could build a skiff cheaper than he could buy, hired a crew and built one. He admitted that it cost him more to buy the material than the boatbuilders of North Bay were charging for the finished skiff.

By 1931 Edward Farrell's son Ernest, at age eighteen, was ready, able, and eager to be more than a workman in the boatbuilding business. Partner Josiah was willing: He paid Edward for half the business so that Edward and son Ernest could build and equip their own facilities. Each continued to build skiffs. Joe

The BETTY COLLIER built at North Bay.

and his youngest son, Jack, taken out of school at age fourteen, worked together for the next six years, at which time Jack took over the business. Others in the village built boats from time to time when the facilities were available, or when they had an order. Alex Strickland built fourteen, Andrew and Frank built eight, Eugene Farrell built eight, and Ern Jones built one. Jack and Bill Farrell built nine, and Jack and Arthur Farrell built six. Bill Farrell built one long-liner.

The First World War had little effect on the young men at North Bay. The small, remote, outport villages five hundred miles from the political activities at Saint John's were of small interest to government officials. Villagers had no interest in the political bickering at Saint John's. French fishermen on the south coast had been squeezed out by the end of the treaty rights, with occasional bloody encounters as the English reclaimed the coastline.

Andrew was first in the village to get a radio, a battery-powered earphone set, in 1925. In 1930 wires connected the village with a Morse code line that bypassed the village on its way over

Max Strickland, Ernest and Arthur Farrell.

the mountain from La Poile to Burgeo. It connected a crank telephone in Edward Farrell's living room with an operator in La Poile. It was, of course, available for use by anyone in the village.

The government began mail service in 1934. Julia Farrell served as postmistress and James Taylor was the mail carrier. The post office was in Josiah's small "store" next to his house.

The water-powered sawmill continued to be used to saw the logs until Josiah purchased the huge gasoline-powered, one-cylinder engine in about 1941. Now they could saw logs at any time of year, summer or winter, without the restrictions caused by lack of a water supply.

The North Bay-built skiffs had multiple uses. The *Ralph and Bob*

Sailboat built by Jack Farrell for Dr. Carden.

was bought by merchant Bob Newman and used as a freighter between Newfoundland and the mainland and south to the States. The *Minnie and Joan* fished the Cape Breton coast. The *Just Righ*t was another fishing boat. The *Debbie and Clara* was a long-liner for coastal fishing. Many of the skiffs in the earlier years undoubtedly made one or more trips "down North" along the Labrador coast with hundreds of other sailing ships that followed the cod migration each summer.

Edward Farrell, before he married, named a skiff he had built after a girlfriend, the *Poppy M*, much to his embarrassment when he married another girl. The *Poppy M* was lost while fishing off the French islands.

The *Mansell and Rita* was a sailing schooner that was engaged in shore fisheries in winter, and in carrying coal from North Sydney and vegetables from Prince Edward Island to the southern ports of Newfoundland in summer. Its half model still decorates a wall in Alec Chant's living room in La Poile. The *Robbie and Brad* was the last long-liner built at North Bay.

Boat by Arthur Farrell to transport sports and supplies.

As evidenced by the number of oceangoing vessels constructed at North Bay, the logging and sawing required to produce the material with which to build them, the guiding, the haying to feed the sheep and oxen, and the hunting and fishing to feed themselves, there was more than enough work to keep the men and older boys busy full time. The quality of construction gained them a good reputation and repeat orders. It was steady work by reliable and experienced men, and they were justifiably proud.

The boys grew into the work of boatbuilding, beginning as errand boys, "gofers," and progressing to experienced workmen while still in their teens. Some left the remote village for Nova Scotia, other parts of Canada, or the United States; but particularly during the early years, most of them either stayed at North Bay or returned after brief trips to the outside.

For the most part, they married girls within the three-family (Strickland, Farrell, Taylor) village or from nearby La Poile, West Point, Rose Blanche, or Grand Bruit; and they stayed at North Bay and raised their families there.

The girls, however, as they became young women, had little future to look forward to at North Bay. With few unrelated men available, and the lack of transportation to even the nearest village of only a hundred or so individuals—and some of them related—local marriage was not a good prospect. Frank Strickland's daughter, Bessie, married Ernest Jones, from Boston, and they lived for some time at North Bay, Ern becoming a boatbuilder. But Bessie appears to have been the exceptional girl to convince an "outsider" (from the States) to move to North Bay.

The alternative was for the young lady to leave North Bay. Josiah's oldest daughter, Minnie, took that route. Edward Farrell had taken in his wife's sister's orphaned son at a young age. He and Minnie became sweethearts, and when of age, the young man left North Bay and settled in Cobourg, Ontario. Minnie had promised to follow him as soon as he got a steady job. After a series of letters between them, on June 3, 1930, Minnie left North Bay and moved to Cobourg. Once there, the ardor cooled. Minnie later married another man and formed the nucleus of what became a considerable group of North Bay young women who migrated to Cobourg, and married and raised their families there, never to return for more than a brief visit.

Though as children the daughters of Josiah and Edward participated in gathering chips and shavings from the boatbuilding area and brought them in baskets and wheelbarrows up to the various homes to fuel the low iron stoves, Dulcie, for one, continued with "men's" work. Somewhat taller and stronger than her sisters and cousins, she was willing and able to pull one end of the crosscut saw. At age twenty, she was as capable as any of the men when swinging an ax to fell trees and chop off the limbs. With a shortage of young men in the village, her help was most welcome.

Haying—the cutting, hauling, and storing of the meadow hay on the river islands for the oxen and sheep—was a family chore rather than "his" or "hers" work.

12

North Bay Immigrants

With a thousand or more of the two-masted forty-five- to sixty-foot-long wooden sailing boats fishing for cod "down north along the Labrador," in addition to their use in "coasting" Newfoundland, Canadian, and United States ports—along with the increased demand for oceangoing vessels during the First World War—the boatbuilders of North Bay experienced a steady demand for their boats. There was no age limit, young or old, that kept physically able men from working. From sweeping away the shavings, carrying the chips to the homes for fuel, and "Bring me my chisel," the boys started as young teens and kept working as long as they could pass a board or drive a nail. But with only two families living at North Bay, the number of available workers was limited.

The nearest settlers lived out the bay about six miles and consisted of several families along the shore of Northeast Bay, at East Bay, and along the western shore of La Poile Bay. Alex Strickland, a young man with a reputation as a good workman (not related to Andrew and Frank), lived at East Bay and was recruited by Josiah and Edward about 1920. As Frank had moved to Boston, Alex moved into the empty house. A romance flourished with Josiah's daughter, Ethel. They were soon married, and soon with children, and became members of the North Bay village. Their son, James, married Patricia, daughter of Edward Farrell.

George Taylor Sr. and his wife, Hannah Neil, lived around the bend from North Bay in East Bay. They had nine children. Like the men at North Bay, George sported a mustache; unlike them, though, he kept it as long as he lived. In the early 1920s he worked part time for the boatbuilders at North Bay, about four miles or so from his home. He was a capable workman and earned steady employment.

In 1926 he moved with his family to North Bay and there built a substantial house on the east side of the river. The couple's first child, Eli, and youngest, Ethel, died very young. Their daughter Louisa never married. Jesse and Percy were young children at the time. His daughter Fanny had married Frederick Strickland. His son Thomas married Dulcie Farrell, daughter of Josiah.

Though the Taylor's and several other families lived at various locations along East Bay, only five or six miles from the village of North Bay, with only rowboat transportation available there was little intimate social connections between them until outboard motors became available and affordable. Their occasional visits occurred when North Bay residents were en route to or from La Poile to buy or sell. The arrival of Alex Strickland and the George Taylor Sr. family from East Bay brought new blood to the village.

The widowed Esther (Essie) Strickland (not related to the North Bay Strickland's) from West Point, sister of Josiah's wife, Julia, moved with her two daughters to keep house for George Taylor Jr. Daughter Violet would marry Percy Taylor, and Hilda later married Max Strickland.

Eugene Farrell had married a daughter of John Strickland (of East Bay) and moved from East Bay to North Bay in 1925. They had six children but separated in 1934. The children stayed with Eugene. Mary, daughter of George Taylor Sr., moved in with Eugene and his children. Eugene and Mary married and had four children.

Arthur and William, sons of Eugene, married Billard sisters from Grand Bruit. They built homes in North Bay and stayed.

13

The Ministers

As the English population migrated easterly down the southern coast of Newfoundland, they populated—at least temporarily—every navigable harbor along the way, even those capable of mooring only rowboats and some within walking distance across a point of land from the next. They replaced the French fishermen who had originally settled in the better harbors, but kept the village names. They gave English names to the previously unnamed harbors such as Stone Harbor, West Point, North Bay, and others in between. The villages were small and were populated by related families that often worked together as a community. Members frequently visited with one another.

They were further united through church affiliation. A visiting minister was assigned each year to make regular trips along the coast. The ministers conducted religious services, baptized the babies, performed the marriages, and officiated at funeral services. The schedule began with a two-week visit at Petites, then to West Point including nearby Stone Harbor, on to La Poile, North Bay, and farther along the coast to Grand Bruit. When the weather or other scheduling problems kept the minister from his appointed visits to North Bay, Thomas Farrell, as a lay minister, conducted the services.

The following is taken from *The United Church Observer*, published in Saint John's in 1948, and written by H. Maxwell Dame, superintendent of missions in Newfoundland.

> The following day, through the kindness of fishing crew, we were given passage to La Poile; and from there we went on to North Bay by motor boat. The service was held that Sat-

urday night in the little church where we met a dedicated and worshipping congregation...as we did again on Sunday morning.

This little community nestling in the bottom of the long arm of La Poile Bay has been the centre of boat building operations on the part of an industrious group of people for a good many years. The timber has been cut, hauled by oxen, and sawn, the boats laid down, ribbed, planked, decked and finished right in the settlement. The whining of the saw, the sound of the caulking hammer and the smell of spruce and balsam greet one as his boat touches the beach and is hauled to safety on the quiet shore.

We stayed the night with Mr. Edward Farrell, whose home is always open to friends of the church as well as to other visitors; and we enjoyed the fellowship in the course of our conversation. I learned that Mr. Farrell had helped to build no less than 200 fishing craft, twenty of which he had completed himself from the chopping of the keel, timbers, and plank out of the trees that grow along the La Poile River to fitting the mast after the boat had been launched into the still waters of the bay. These small auxiliary schooners go by the names of "western fishing boats" and are found to be very practical in the cod, herring, and salmon fisheries which in season are carried on all the year round along the southwest coast. Salmon fishery was carried out in June and July. They (the boats) are sometimes fitted out for sword fishing, a very exciting, and if successful, profitable undertaking.

Among the group of that now rapidly dwindling community are two great Christian souls, long past their active labours through age and infirmity, Thomas Farrell and wife Rachel.

The ministers who made these scheduled visits to the remote villages along the coast were more familiar than any other outsider with the intimate activities of the settlements. They were greeted at the beach in summer and met at the edge of the bay ice in winter, always welcome. They preached in the churches, the schoolhouses, and not unusually in a parishioner's living room before more suitable facilities were available.

In their church papers, they also recorded many of their observations and experiences, some of which describe the dangers to which they were often exposed. The following is one example (also written by H. Maxwell Dame).

> Indeed, there is scarcely a cottage that had not been visited; and as we came in sight of the houses of Stone Harbor we recalled again the tragedy that had overtaken my predecessor, Rev. Oliver Jackson and his companion, Mr. Wallace Harris, ten years before on that gray November morning when they had passed through the floodgates of death unto eternal life as the breaking waves dashed their small craft upon the goring reef. We landed on the desolate shore for a few moments to view the wreckage that is still there, a boat's prow now upturned like some memorial stone, just beyond the high water mark; and as I stood with my companion listening to the wind fitfully ruffling the white foam, I recalled again what someone had said, "God buries His workmen and carries on His work."
>
> That night the congregation from Stone Harbor, West Point, and Indian Harbor gathered with us in reverence and humility to worship God. We met crowded together in the tiny weather-beaten schoolroom and not in the church where Oliver Jackson and Wallace Harris had held their last service, for since my previous visit there came a dreadful night when the deep waters of the South Atlantic had again rolled shoreward in cruel foam, lashed into relentless fury by the winds which blew out of the rainy darkness. The storm beat upon little boats and the little homes and upon the church. In the morning the villagers looked out to find that the place where they went to pray had been demolished, and they have not yet found the resources to rebuild the House of God.

The village of North Bay, nine miles from the open ocean up a relatively narrow bay and between mountains more than a thousand feet high, was afforded considerable protection from the storms that caused havoc in the smaller coastal harbors. But being so remote exposed residents more to the hazards of accidents and illness, and to weather conditions that kept them isolated for days at a time.

14

Josiah and Julia

The advantages of even so small a change as that required of operating the water-powered circular saw in place of the two-man pitsaw were somewhat diminished when Josiah, whose idea and construction were responsible for it, had a careless moment. He put his hand onto the whirling blade. Suddenly he was bleeding profusely from deep cuts on the inside of every finger on his left hand. An inch of the little finger hung loosely by a thin ribbon of skin and flesh.

Quickly, Julia applied a tourniquet above her husband's elbow to slow the bleeding, washed the cuts in a pan of boiled water taken from the kettle on the stove, and carefully wrapped each finger. She replaced the unattached little finger as well and bound it tightly to the next finger. The splice was successful, though the finger remained slightly bent and always sensitive to the cold.

To be able to react quickly to such emergencies was a matter of course for the village women. It was their responsibility also to be prepared for any family health problem that was not serious enough to get the patient to a doctor, who was more than fifty miles away in Port aux Basques. Each family had a limited number of patent medicines, including Brick's Tasteless Cod Liver Oil and Ginger Wine. They kept a bottle of brandy on hand. They made a bitter drink by steeping the inside bark of a cherry tree and used this to cure a cold or "not feeling well" situation. They collected a ground juniper with its berries from the highland and steeped it for stomach or bowel problems. And the women exchanged secret concoctions for treating other symptoms. Babies were born without benefit of a doctor.

Josiah (Joe) Farrell and Julia (Stone) Farrell, wife of Joe.

By 1920, and until he moved away, Josiah had the only store in the village. He kept a limited variety of groceries, nails, cloth, and whatever other items his neighbors might need—actually, a surplus of his own goods. When mail service became available and his wife, Julia, was appointed postmistress, the post office was in the store.

With a family of nine children, it was understandable that Josiah and Julia would experience their full share of sorrows.

In midwinter of 1934, their son Cecil, then twenty years old, suddenly became ill. He did not respond to the usual home remedies and the family realized that a doctor was needed. A call was made on the recently installed (1930) telephone to Julia's brothers at West Point. The brothers left promptly in a forty-two-foot, two-masted fishing boat in the face of a brewing storm and met members of the family, who brought Cecil out from the bay to the edge of the ice. Back at West Point, the storm was too severe to continue toward Port aux Basques that night; and the rough weather did not stop for the next two days. Cecil died of a burst appendix at about the time they got him to the doctor at Port aux Basques.

Six years later, in February 1940, their next oldest son, Leslie, was taken to Sydney, Nova Scotia, and operated on at the hospital there for an improperly healed broken foot. Back at North Bay, the foot became infected. Further observation revealed a piece of gauze that had been accidentally left inside during the operation. Leslie returned to the hospital in Sydney, where the gauze was removed and the wound treated. But he was then diagnosed with appendicitis and underwent an operation from which he did not recover. An autopsy revealed other internal problems that caused his death.

Seven years later, in 1947, Julia became ill. She died then at age fifty-seven.

Josiah continued in his small workshop, building and selling rowboats. He later remarried and eventually retired. He moved to Ontario to be near his daughter Minnie and other members of his family. He made several visits back to North Bay before he died at age ninety-one.

15

The Village

From midwife-assisted births to puberty, children of various ages outnumbered the adults. Pearl reflected her father Josiah's frustration and probably her own in writing that he must have been discouraged when girl after girl was born. His wife gave him six daughters and only three sons, two of whom died in early maturity.

Of the thirteen families living at North Bay at its peak of population (between 1907 and 1953), apparently members of each family contributed to the building of boats. Each family had several children with no school building until 1914. The care for, entertainment, and teaching of children from diaper to fishing and embroidering ages persisted in the winter as well as in summer. Each of the houses had been built with the expectation of large families or many guests. Each was two stories, with four or more bedrooms and a large kitchen dominated by a low iron stove with a high oven heated by exhaust through the stovepipe before it entered the chimney. Chips and shavings contributed fuel for heat and cooking both summer and winter.

Christmas and birthday presents usually consisted of home-knitted clothes, from gloves to socks, from hats to sweaters. Toys, from sailboats to dolls, were homemade by the older men when they were unable to do physical work. The older women knitted and watched the babies while the babies' mothers did the cooking and the menial chores associated with toiletries without running water and outhouses some distance from the homes.

Once ambulatory, the small children of the large families and often those of the near neighbors were mostly cared for by the older children. An older girl was usually experienced in caring for babies and small children long before she married and left home.

There was no need or use of roads, and there were none. Footpaths connected the houses, the outhouses, the boat shops, and sawmill. The "lawn" between was "mowed" by sheep. The path to the river was trodden through the tall grass and low alders by those who went up the river to fish (or in summer to swim and bathe). The logs left no marks below the snow or ice when dragged by oxen on the frozen river or carried by the spring flush of the flowing current.

There was no government, as such, at North Bay: no mayor, constable, postmistress (until 1934), or tax collector. There was no need for them. More like one big family than a village, problems between individuals were worked out before they got to the boiling point. Throughout the period, Andrew Strickland seems to have been the patriarchal figure. Without being in any way officious, he just always was there in the background when needed. Josiah Farrell, on the other hand, was the village leader, the man with ideas who got things done, such as constructing the model by which to build his skiffs, building the sluice and the water-powered sawmill, rigging a hull when it could not be sold as it was, and sailing it to demonstrate its seaworthiness in order to sell it.

16

Early Sport Guiding

Wildlife was plentiful in the La Poile River valley and on the nearby mountains, and provided much of the food when the Strickland's and the Farrell's settled at North Bay. The native caribou fed on the tundralike mountains in winter, came into the valley in spring, and in summer came to shallow water at low tide for the salt in kelp and sea grass.

Andrew and Frank Strickland, and Thomas Farrell with his older sons, Reuben and Josiah, also hunted ptarmigan and ducks and caught cod, salmon, and trout in season. The families preserved both meat and fish in glass jars, salted and smoked and dried, to extend the seasonal supplies. They also trapped, selling furs to the Hudson's Bay Company. Their traplines reached far over the mountains. Base lean-to shelters were built where they might stay for several days and nights while making sets and reaping the catch. They skinned the carcasses of fox, muskrat, lynx, and otter before moving on to another lean-to in a fresh area. After two weeks or more in the bush, living mostly off the land, they would backpack the hides to the village, there to be stretched and dried. The trappers went on the longer trips in pairs, usually a father and teenage son or an older and younger brother.

These experiences brought a knowledge of the wildlife and terrain helpful not only in their efforts to obtain food but also to guide others in pursuit of meat and trophies. There were few "sports" to guide during the early years. Other than the natives who fished and hunted for their own food, the first to come to North Bay to hunt caribou or to cast flies for salmon may have

Jean Farrell and Bill Farrell on their way to build a new hunting camp on the high land.

been men who grew up there but moved away at a young age, and who came back to visit relatives. And they may have included the buyers who came to take possession of the boats built at the village. They stayed with Andrew or Frank Strickland and were taken on day trips up the valley to hunt or to the lower river pools to fish. Once exposed to the thrills and excitement of catching salmon on rod and reel—even with the twelve-foot, double-handed, stiff, greenheart wooden rods and the cotton lines and gut leaders used by the first fly fishermen—they were sure to come back for more. And they brought friends—ship captains and the importers in Canada and the United States to whom the captains delivered their cargoes. Some of them became paying customers for board and room and hunting or fishing guiding.

The guides cooked the meals, washed the dishes, and showed the sports where and how to catch the salmon. The names of some of these early fishermen still survive in Squire's Flat, for example, where the individual came for a period long enough to have the area named for him. And Gosse's Pool still bears his

name, although the person responsible is long forgotten. There are other "flats," pools, and crossings named for those who for one reason or another became associated with them.

After Frank Strickland and his family moved to Boston, he frequently returned to indulge in his love of hunting and fishing, and he was responsible for bringing some of the first sportfishermen from the United States. Andrew was the first to guide them. They brought their "cotton camps" and spent a week or more camping on the split river's grassy islands while fishing for salmon. Andrew built a rude camp on the west side of Lower Salmon Brook Pool, an overnight habitation for the more aggressive fishermen. Soon these sports were coming in the fall. They'd stay ten nights in lean-to shelters on the highlands to hunt for trophy caribou, with Frederick Strickland and Edward Farrell as guides.

A story persists of a North Bay hunter who shot a trophy whose antlers had fifty points.

The caribou population reached a peak in about 1915 and was reduced drastically during the next fifteen years. The cause was due in part to excessive legal and illegal hunting. The wolves in Newfoundland had been exterminated by 1911. However, because the Canadian hare, until then the primary food for lynx, had reached a very low population level, the lynx concentrated on caribou for their major source of food and came close to exterminating them before their own population was reduced by starvation.

Older residents of North Bay remembered male caribou weighing up to five hundred pounds before the near extinction and noted that the males in the present population would weigh about one hundred pounds. This suggests that the government may have imported some of the smaller woodland caribou to help increase the population, but no such program has been confirmed. Natives suggested that both strains may have existed on the mainland at the same (prehistoric) time, before Newfoundland became an island; or that one or both may have crossed on the ice during years when the Strait of Belle Isle froze. According to Jack Farrell, it was reported that at some time a lumber com-

Jack Farrell with his and Percy Taylor's oxen packing supplies to hunting camp.

pany on the north shore brought in twenty reindeer (a smaller caribou) with a herdsman from Lapland, with the intent of using them in logging operations during the winter. When it was determined that the project was not practical, the herd was turned loose. Perhaps these animals survived and reproduced, and even interbred with the local population.

Both Frederick Strickland and Edward Farrell became active in guiding sport hunters from Port aux Basques, the United States, and the Canadian provinces in their quest to obtain trophies and meat. During the peak of this seasonal occupation, Strickland and Farrell each had built several hunting cabins in caribou-favored locations on the mountains.

They not only guided the hunters, but they also carried in the supplies and carried out the meat and trophies. After Frank Strickland initiated the use of a pack saddle on his ox in 1916, which had worked so well for getting supplies up the river for the men cutting logs, other members of the community pur-

chased pack saddles, and the oxen were used to pack in supplies and to bring out trophies.

Guiding for caribou hunts was reduced as the herd was reduced. It ended when the government stopped issuing licenses, from 1924 to 1934.

Two moose, a bull and a cow, had been brought to Newfoundland from Nova Scotia and released in the area near Gander in 1878. In 1904 four cows and three bull moose were trapped at Miramichi in New Brunswick. Three died during a delay in transportation at North Sydney, but the remaining two bulls and two cows were released in Howley, near Grand Lake. It appears that progeny of both immigrations of the moose survived, though it was estimated that no more than eleven could have been alive (and fewer seen) by 1912. However, they were reported seen as far away as the south shore at Grand Bruit in 1934, and by 1944 had become quite common throughout Newfoundland.

As the number of moose increased, the number of illegally killed caribou decreased; with the wolves exterminated and the number of lynx considerably reduced, caribou numbers began a slow rise. And what appears to have been a generous allocation of moose permits to natives also kept moose-poaching to a minimum.

Though seasonal and usually extending only for six weeks or so each fall, the hunting for trophies and meat brought outside cash to the village from well-to-do and generous sports. Sport hunting, and therefore guiding, was considerably reduced during the period (1924-1934) when no licenses to hunt caribou were issued and before the moose population had reached acceptable numbers; but hunting for both species was revived by the mid-thirties.

While hunting season occurred too late for the salmon run in the La Poile River, the hunters may well have feasted on sea-run trout or even an occasional salmon during their overnight stays at North Bay. It appears that some, if not many, of those sports who came to hunt for moose and caribou returned the next spring to catch salmon from the river.

17

Frank Strickland's Boat Fire

Frank Strickland often returned to North Bay from his home and boatbuilding work in Boston to visit relatives and friends. In 1932 he built a sixty-five-foot motor vessel, the *Edith Cavelle,* loaded a hundred barrels of gasoline, brought the cargo to Newfoundland, and sold it, some there at North Bay. He returned to Boston in the fall, leaving the schooner moored at La Poile. He returned the next spring, moved the vessel to an anchorage off the cemetery at Jimmy's Place, built a large wooden tank in the hull, and filled it with salt water from the ocean, intending to purchase lobsters to fill it and take them to Boston to sell.

With preparations complete and ready to leave the next morning, they filled the fuel tank with gasoline—in fact they overfilled and spilled some in the process—before covering the hatches for the night.

Before they had the anchor pulled and the vessel underway the next morning, a spark from the engine ignited gasoline fumes that had accumulated in the hull during the night. There was a terrific explosion and fire and the *Edith Cavelle* sank in shallow water not far from shore. No one was killed in the accident, but several on board were badly burned. They were taken to the hospital in Port aux Basques, where they stayed for some time. They were then nursed by relatives at North Bay until they healed sufficiently to return to Boston.

The hull was refloated and towed to a cove near the Jimmy's Place cemetery in North Bay, where it remained for four years. Then Frank returned, got help, and floated and towed it to North Bay, where it was hauled onto the shore toward the boat shops.

The boatbuilders went to work and rebuilt the ship. Launched there at North Bay, Frank again built a large wooden tank in the hull and filled it with sea water. At villages along the coast he purchased lobsters, and the full cargo was finally taken to Boston and sold.

Frank later built another boat in Boston and sailed it in the passenger service in the Florida Keys.

18

The Boatbuilder's Village

The era of boatbuilding at North Bay extended from 1892 until about 1960, after which time only Jack Farrell, with cousin Arthur or William, built at least seven long-liners and one or more smaller boats. Boats were recorded as having been built by one or more individuals, but these names identified the people who financed and managed the building, not the actual workers.

Prior to 1926, when George Taylor Sr. moved his family from Northwest Cove on East Bay to North Bay, although he and/or members of his family may have worked on the boats at North Bay at times, the village population consisted of the descendants of John Strickland and Thomas Farrell.

Andrew Strickland had built the first house on the high ground well up from the river and near the Drinking Brook which tumbled from the thousand-foot mountain in a series of falls to the beginning of the slight slope a hundred yards beyond and southerly of the house and through a gully to where the La Poile River meets the bay.

Andrew's house, like most of the original homes built slightly later, was of two stories with four or more second-story bedrooms (with expectation of large families or room for overnight visitors). Frank built down the slope a hundred feet or so and a similar distance to the east. They cut and hewed the sills and other timbers from fir and spruce and pit-sawed the boards to enclose and roof the houses.

The third house, also large and with two stories, was that of Thomas Farrell, whose nine children at the time they moved from East Bay certainly filled the house; he built directly behind

Boat built by Jack and Arthur Farrell circa 1947.

Andrew's house, well back and close to where Drinking Brook landed from its plunge down the mountain. Within the next ten years, Thomas's son Josiah married (Julia Stone) and built a home of his own, another large two-story house some seventy-five feet to the east of his father's house and straight back on the slope from Frank's house.

Josiah's brother, Edward, married Annie Anderson and built on a small level bank close to where the La Poile River meets the low tide, across Drinking Brook from the other houses. And as the children of Andrew Strickland and the younger children of Josiah Farrell came of age, houses were built by Albert Strickland, Eugene Farrell, and Alexander Strickland (not related to Andrew), whose son, James, married Edward Farrell's daughter Patricia. These ten buildings comprised the village of North Bay and provided the manpower (and womanpower) of North Bay until George Taylor Sr. moved there in 1926. The schoolhouse had been built in about 1914 between the homes of Andrew and Thomas and close to the bank of the narrow "valley" of Drinking Brook.

The sawmill stood opposite the schoolhouse. The two large workshops of Josiah and Edward-Ernest, in which boats up to

Boat built by Arthur Farrell after he retired at age 77.

sixty feet long were built, and several barns for the cows, oxen, and their hay were also in the small valley of Drinking Brook.

Tenants changed as the years passed and the elders died or moved away: Andrew's house went to his grandson Max, Thomas Farrell's to Percy Taylor, Josiah's to son Jack, Eugene's to son Arthur, Frank Strickland's to Frederick Strickland to Duncan Smith, and Edward Farrell's to his nephew William.

A study of the genealogy of these families shows that the numbers of working men—boatbuilders and guides—peaked after the Taylor's moved to North Bay and Ern Jones from Boston married Andrew's daughter Bessie, making a total population of about fifty individuals in a dozen homes, including three on the east side of the river.

A list of the boats built with the individual(s) responsible and the period of years for each provides considerable information as to the level of boatbuilding activity as it took place between 1892 and 1968:

Number Built	*Name of Builder(s)*	*Years in which Built*
4	Thomas Farrell	1892-1903
8	Andrew and Frank Strickland	1895-1912
46	Josiah and Edward Farrell	1903-1921
36	Josiah Farrell	1921-1936
20	Edward and Ernest Farrell	1921-1936
8	Eugene Farrell	1920-1940
14	Alex Strickland	1926-1942
9	Jack and Bill Farrell	1946-1953
1	Ern Jones	1940-1942
1	William Farrell	1955-1957
6	Jack and Arthur Farrell	1955-1968

Boats built before Josiah designed and built the waterpower mill on Drinking Brook (1951) went from growing trees to marketed ships using hand tools only.

Half model of the Mansell and Rita *is mounted on the living room wall at the home of Alec and Eilene Chant in La Poile and was provided to them by Ernest Farrell. The 60-foot long liner was built by Jack and Arthur Farrell in 1968, the last ship built at North Bay.*

19

The Bob Pike Era

In the late 1930s, motor trouble left Bob Pike and his salmon-fishing friend, Dr. Verne Schaffner, adrift near the entrance to North Bay. This marked the beginning of a fifty-year history of guiding sportfishermen on the La Poile River.

Bob Pike was a successful businessman in Port aux Basques. He also enjoyed fishing for salmon. During the season, he made many trips easterly along the south shore in his motorboat at least as far as the Conne River to cast his flies. When his two daughters were diagnosed with tuberculosis, he had them admitted to the highly recommended TB sanitarium in Kentville, Nova Scotia, sold his business, and retired to Kentville to be near them. He soon became acquainted with Dr. Verne Schaffner, chief surgeon at the institution, and also a fly-fishing enthusiast. The two were soon making annual trips to Newfoundland to fish Pike's familiar rivers.

Unable to start their motor when it failed in La Poile Bay, Pike and Schaffner accepted an offer of a tow from a friendly North Bay native who was returning from a visit to La Poile and suggested that someone at the village could repair the motor. While waiting for the repair work to be completed, Pike and Schaffner cast their flies on the La Poile River with some success and vowed to return. Following subsequent trips to North Bay and expert guiding by Frederick Strickland, Pike hired Fred to build a cabin for him on the high bank close to Salmon Hole Pool. That summer, in the late 1930s, when the bark would peel clean from the fir logs, Frederick, with his teenage son, Max, and another helper went the three miles upriver and cleared the bank beside

Soup party at Violet and Percy Taylor's, about 1935. From left: Bill and Lucy Farrell, Hilda Strickland, Henry Farrell, Harold Melbourne, Percy Taylor, Ernest Farrell, Fred Strickland, and Tom Farrell. Children in background: Audrey and Lois.

Salmon Hole Pool, cut the necessary trees, stripped the bark from the logs, and built a cabin about twelve by sixteen feet. Then, or in early following years, they added a small, separate cooking-dining building and another, smaller cabin for the guides' sleeping quarters.

Pike and Schaffner came to the cabin each year to fish and hunt. The first years of their annual trips to North Bay emphasized caribou and moose hunting, two weeks in the fall in the remote camps on the mountains and one week in the spring at Salmon Hole cabin to fish. During that time they added Ian Baird, also from Kentville, to the party. After several years of fruitless persuasion, they finally convinced Dr. Horace Foley to end his eleven years of unbroken medical service to his community and join them on their annual vacations to North Bay. He had been available all hours of the day, seven days a week and every day of the year. Dr. Foley was ready to "let down his hair." The others were already experienced in participating in at least

Edith and Reuben Farrell at cabin built by Salmon Hole Pool on the LaPoile.

one good drunk following the rigors of the trip: hiking first the three rocky miles from North Bay to the Salmon Hole cabin for a night, then up the mountain to the high ground the next day to a second rough camp in the hunting area. There the two weeks provided plenty of time for "relaxing" as well as hunting. The guides accompanied them—Frederick Strickland, Edward Farrell, and often Percy Taylor or others who were available—with the oxen trailing with food and supplies in saddlebags. There were no schedules, no appointments to keep. The meals were cooked and served and the dishes washed by guides who were capable of handling any circumstance, from patience required on "morning afters" to taking the hunters to within shooting distance of caribou and moose with trophy antlers.

For another decade or so, there were few if any other annual hunting or fishing parties for the guides of North Bay. There was no ferry transportation beyond where the road from Port aux Basques ended at Rose Blanche. There was only a freight service, which ran without a firm schedule about once a week. The sportsmen made arrangements ahead of time for the guides or local fishermen to meet and transport them from Rose Blanche to North Bay; and it was not unusual that, due to fog or other weather conditions, trips were delayed, sometimes for several days. There were other hunting areas and other rivers far more accessible to sportsmen and with trophy caribou and moose in good numbers; and few sportsmen had ever heard of the La Poile River. Hunting and fishing in the La Poile River valley was left pretty much to natives of the area and to the parties from Nova Scotia. And the natives were thankful to let it remain that way.

Pike gave Frederick Strickland use of the cabin while guiding other parties when Pike and his party were not there in return for being cabin caretaker. Fred jealously protected the property and the river to the extent of allowing few others the use of it. After Fred died, a native was heard to comment, "Now he dead. The devil got he. River still there."

Though only seasonally, and not always a full season and with varying numbers of sports, the hunting and fishing guiding gradually increased in economic importance to those in the village. The Kentville, Nova Scotia, parties dominated. As increased from only Pike and Schaffner to as many as six hunters or fishermen, other North Bay natives also guided.

The "reign" of Bob Pike ended with his death while on a fishing trip to the Conne River during the 1960s. Dr. Schaffner carried on, though growing old, still addicted to the salmon fishing, the natural beauty of the La Poile River valley, and love and respect for the people of North Bay.

Though not the first, Max Strickland was appointed River Guardian for the La Poile. For many years he kept neat and complete records of those who fished the river.

20

Andrew's Accident

Too many epitaphs in the family trees of the residents of North Bay read "died young" to indicate a lack of intimacy with death. Without an accurate diagnosis of appendicitis in time to get the patient to the nearest hospital, death was the result during what seemed like an epidemic of the disease in one family. Occasionally the midwifery and lack of a doctor for young children ended in deaths that might have been avoided under other circumstances.

The lack of accidents in the workplace, however, shows that the boatbuilders, the loggers, and those pulling the pit saws were respectful of their tools and used them properly. Despite every precaution, however, accidents did happen, even to the most careful.

Not long after Edward Farrell had taken his young son, Ernest, as partner in boatbuilding, the two were working from a staging on the high sides of an unfinished hull. From his position one side of the boat, Ernest heard a crash. He rushed to the other side to find that his father had fallen from the ten-foot stage onto a pile of lumber. Edward was fortunate: He suffered no more than two broken ribs in the fall, but recovery was slow and the pain kept him from work for several weeks. Ernest worked extra hours to complete the boat.

Albert Strickland, son of Andrew, had agreed to do some repair work on the fishing schooner. It was sailed up the bay to the workshop launching site and grounded at high tide in the mouth of the river where ships built in the shops were launched. With the bow of the boat upstream, its position was at an angle from

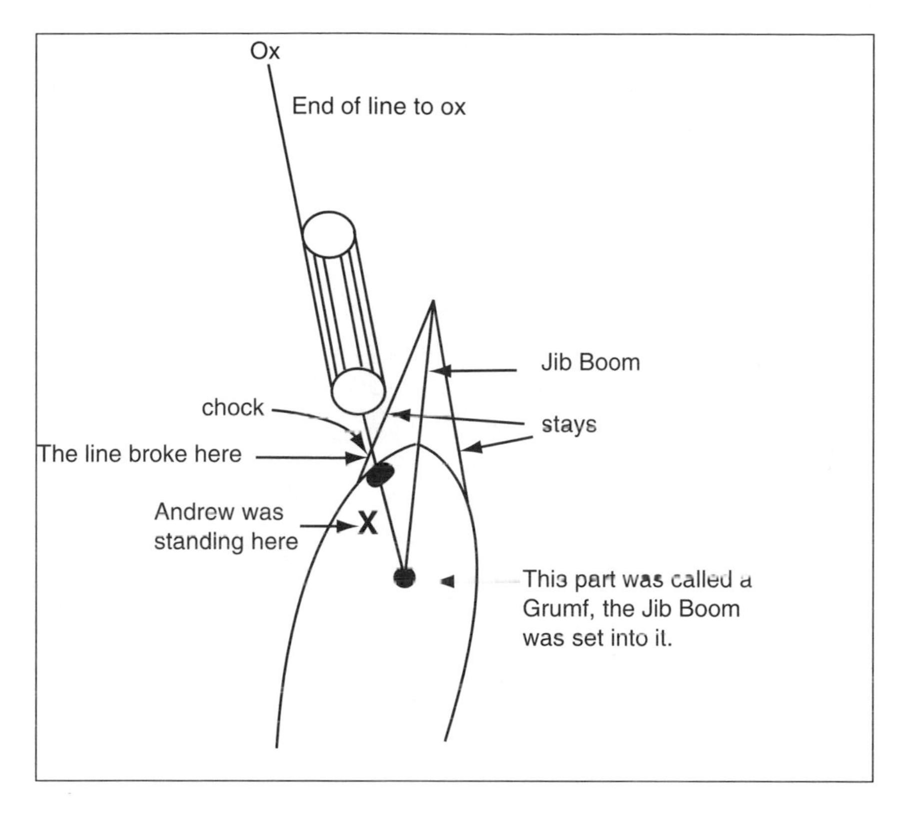

Diagram of Andrew's accident.

the pulling point and the boat itself tipped somewhat to port as the tide receded.

The pulling hawser was attached to the grumf post. Andrew carried it forward and placed it in the rouse chock near the bow. A young lad, son of the boat owner, had followed Andrew as he attached the hawser and carried it forward. Apparently recognizing the danger that the hawser might slip out of the chock or that the chock could break from the pressure applied by the pull, Andrew sent the boy aft to midship before giving the signal for the ox to begin pulling on the tackle. Andrew himself stepped back only a few feet.

Due to the somewhat uphill pull of the hawser to the bow of the boat, a break of the rouse chock or to some other reason, the chock failed to hold. Under great pressure the hawser broke or snapped from its position in the choke and hit Andrew in the head with a riflelike crack. Andrew was killed instantly, his body knocked off the bow of the boat and into the water below. His son Albert got to him quickly in a rowboat with one push of the oars, grabbed his father's face-down body by the belt, and with one hand lifted him into the boat. Others were there to take him from the rowboat to Edward Farrell's house nearby, where the stunned group came to realize the extent of the sudden tragedy.

One moment Andrew Strickland, pioneer settler of North Bay, on October 20, 1943, at age sixty-seven, was doing the routine work along with his sons, brother, relatives and friends–the work he had done all of his life–the next, he was dead.

Andrew was buried in the small, white-picket-fence-enclosed lot where his mother had been buried only four years earlier. He remains on the land granted to him and his brother Frank, the land they had cleared on the knoll above where the La Poile River meets the head of the long bay, on which he had built the first house, a home in which he and his family had lived for fifty years.

Andrew's death came at a time when the village was at its peak of boatbuilding production and its peak population of about fifty residents. The Second World War had extended the otherwise reduced demand for wooden boats.

21

The Fire at North Bay

For two days before May 13, 1953, a strong wind, gusting to fifty miles per hour, had blown up the bay, across the launching area, between and over the ox barns, the sawmill, the workshop, up the steep bank and dug-in vegetable cellars and past the schoolhouse, through the village. The wind was so strong that for the first time since it had been built, the roof blew off Josiah's vegetable cellar. He promptly replaced it, but within an hour it had blown off again. Thinking that the headers to which the roof was fastened might have rotted, he decided to wait until the wind had stopped blowing before rebuilding.

One ox, resting from dragging logs to the sawmill all day, was in the barn nervously shaking his head and shifting uneasily on his feet, leaning from side to side in response to the whistle of the wind and the clatter of a loose shingle.

Another day of building boats had ended at North Bay. The workmen and boys left their tools to be handy to start up the next morning. With the wind at their backs, they walked up past the vegetable cellars along the bank to their various homes, Josiah Farrell's, Percy Taylor's, and Max Strickland's, the schoolhouse between the latter two, in anticipation of hearty meals waiting on hot stoves.

Hardly into the meal, Percy Taylor thought he smelled smoke and got up from his chair at the table to look outside. His shouts brought everyone out of every house to see flames leaping up the side of the sawmill building, a scant fifty feet from the Taylor doorstep and schoolhouse.

The fire fed fiercely on the dry timber, the shavings, and saw-

Buildings at North Bay before the fire.

dust. With the wind so strong, the buildings so close, the fire spread quickly to workshops and barns, leaving no time to save the tools or free the ox. They used their wooden buckets to carry water up the hill from the river, and from Drinking Brook, to throw against the sides of the schoolhouse and the Taylor home as the windows cracked and broke from the intense heat. The children, three of them babies wrapped in blankets, were taken to the river crossing, where they huddled together under the watchful eyes of older sisters and weary, frightened grandmothers while all able-bodied individuals fought to keep embers and heat from igniting their houses. Had the vegetable cellar roof been replaced, it would have been a route for the fire over the steep bank to the schoolhouse, from there to the Taylor house and the rest of the village. Without that link—because Josiah had delayed replacing the blown-off roof—the villagers were able to save their homes.

During the melee, few of the firefighters escaped burns from flying embers as they took turns removing furniture and belongings from the houses to safety and throwing buckets of water, carried on the run, onto the blistering buildings. Propelled by the strong wind gusts, the sawmill and the two large workshops—

Same area after the fire.

the first built by Josiah and the second by Edward—the ox barns, one with an ox inside, and smaller shops burned quickly. When the flames subsided, the stunned villagers stood among their homes in a red glow of sawdust and hay that burned for days.

Their homes—a miracle, it seemed to most—remained intact except for broken windows on the side toward the fire of those nearest the conflagration. But the houses stood in half a village. Their tools, except for the few left upriver where they had been working, and the buildings in which they had built their boats, including one half-finished skiff, were gone. It was a disaster.

One hammer did survive. One of the men had taken it home that noon to repair a clothesline that the wind had broken the night before.

22

End of Boat Building at North Bay

Only four years before the fire, Joseph W. Smallwood, premier of Newfoundland, after years of government consideration, bickering, politicking, and changes of opinions, direction, and leadership, had finally brought about federation of Newfoundland-Labrador with Canada. The government in England had been unable or unwilling to provide satisfactory supervision or protection and was anxious to be rid of the problem, willing to lend its influence toward federation. The Saint John's businessman Chesley A. Crosbie had won little support for his promotion that Newfoundland apply to the United States for statehood, and Newfoundland was financially unable to go it alone. There was really no choice but to accept federation.

The troubled government's problems were of little interest or significance to the population of the small and remote but self-sustaining outport at North Bay. The village got along without any supervision. The government, having settled the treaty rights with the French on the South shore, was satisfied to let sleeping dogs lie for the time being.

But after the catastrophic fire, the boatbuilders of North Bay applied for a government grant with which to rebuild and to replace their tools. They were offered a loan at six percent interest. Rather than go into debt for the three thousand dollars required, Josiah offered the same amount to back his son Jack with cousins Bill and Art. They rebuilt the sawmill and furnished it with a gasoline motor and saws. They added a workshop smaller than those that burned. They used the motor from Arthur's new washing machine to turn out forty 4 inch by 30 inch hard wood rollers on which to move the logs through the board

School children, Verna, Dorothy and Melvin, Joan and Lois.

School children, Lucy, Evelyn, Shirley, Patsy, Uncle Sid, Thelma, Lois, Verna, May, Melvin, Dot, Andrew, Barb, Golda, Norman, Joan, Gordon

North Bay house built by Eugene Farrell.

saw. At the end of a year, Jack and Arthur Farrell started building boats again. They built six long-liners in the next ten years.

Tom Farrell, son of Eugene, living in Rose Blanche, guided fishing parties into the area. By 1960 he hired his wife's brother, Alec Chant, to help.

During the late 1960s the government sent a survey crew to North Bay to make the first topographic maps (prints dated 1985) of the inland area. Jack worked for them for several years. When that was finished, he worked for a crew moving mining equipment onto the mountain out of East Bay. When that was finished, he worked for them in Bathhurst, New Brunswick, then for the provincial government before returning eight years later to the North Bay area. Arthur had moved with his family to Grand Bruit.

But the period of boatbuilding at North Bay was coming to an end. The virgin timber, what little of it was left, was fifteen or more miles up the valley—far from any reasonable method of transportation to the village. The price was much too high to purchase milled lumber from outside sources; and the skiffs and long-liners had been replaced by diesel-powered steel vessels. Some of the young men, including Ernest and Arthur Farrell and Max Strickland, spent time in military service. Villagers had been

Eugene Farrell with grandson.

leaving to accept higher-paying jobs at the paper mills in Newfoundland or had gone to other Canadian provinces even before the government offered incentives to leave. Those not owning land, and therefore qualifying for the two-thousand-dollar incentive to move, now left.

Josiah, by age sixty-three, had lost two sons, one at age twenty, the other at age twenty-four, and his wife at age fifty-seven. He had turned his boatbuilding business over to his remaining son, Jack, then twenty years of age. Josiah built a smaller workshop and for the next two decades built smaller boats, rowboats, then moved to Ontario.

Max Strickland left the house his grandfather Andrew had built and moved his family to Petites in 1966. The George Taylor Jr. family left during the summer of 1968. Only Ernest Farrell remained. Ernest had purchased the big workshop from Jack and bought and remodeled the schoolhouse, in which he lived. He was reluctant to leave; but with no one else there to spend the winter, it would not be wise for him to remain at North Bay alone. He left on November 28, 1968, and moved to Cobourg, Ontario, to be near other members of his family.

He, his brother-in-law James, and James's father, Alexander, visited North Bay during summer vacations. Ernest worked with James in Ontario at construction for several years, for a mobile home company for a couple of years, and did odd jobs until he retired in 1978. He then regularly returned to North Bay during the summer. He activated the sawmill and sawed a season peak of twenty thousand board feet of logs for local sale, including to Percy Taylor and the others who built cottages in the village. He built a table saw using a ten-horsepower, air-cooled motor with which to saw out laths for building lobster pots, selling twenty-two thousand one summer. Max Strickland, then River Guardian, and his family also began spending summers at North Bay, and Max worked regularly with Ernest at the mill until 1995.

By 1968 the last residents had left North Bay. The government paid them to move, all but those on the Strickland and Farrell granted land; and the winter of 1968 was the first since 1890 that the chimney smoke from the woodstoves of the two-story houses did not rise above the village. The ancient one-cylinder gasoline engine that had produced the power to run the saw to saw the logs to build the boats was quiet. There were no sounds of hammering, no boats being built in the workshops, no boats on the way, no men with oxen logging upriver.

But North Bay would not die; or at least it would have a rebirth, but one not including boatbuilding.

As the boatbuilding activities at the village were reduced, Edward Farrell and Frederick Strickland had provided seasonal work for themselves and the other men who remained by guiding caribou and moose hunters and salmon fishermen. They used the oxen to transport food and supplies to their camps on the highland and to bring back the trophies and meat for the hunters until Jack Farrell took over the hunter guiding.

The salmon and char still migrated up the river each summer.

Arthur Farrell roasting a trout.

Frederick Strickland had off and on gradually increased his clientele of sportfishermen from those who years before had stayed at his house to those who stayed in the cotton camps. Now, for the most part, he guided the Pike parties, who spent a week or more at the log cabin three miles up the river on the bank above Salmon Hole Pool.

The second-growth spruce and fir, were now nearing saw log size. An occasional huge, grotesque silver birch not having been long or straight enough to make a keel or planking for ships, and therefore spared by the loggers many years before, spread their millions of seeds; and thick growth beneath was pruned each year by moose when the leaves were lush and green. The sightings of big bulls with massive antlers influenced summer fishermen to return for fall hunting; but the numbers of sport hunters dwindled due to competition from other, more accessible hunt-

Arthur Farrell's sons, Gordon and Keith,
Jack's son Melvin and Max

ing areas of Newfoundland and to the emphasis on salmon fishing by the sports from Nova Scotia.

Frederick's house at North Bay became the way-stop for fishing parties going up the river when tide or weather or transportation problems made an overnight stay necessary. Frederick became caretaker for the Salmon Hole cabin. He made repairs when needed, such as after a black bear visited the cabin in search of food, entered by the window in spite of iron bars, and left by the door. Frederick realized later that leaving the door open saved both the window and the door with no increase in vandalism.

23

Moose Hunt with Oxen

Following the disastrous fire of 1953, some of the workmen who stayed in the village took a more active part in guiding caribou and moose hunters. Not only the fire but also the decreased demand for wooden boats forced a change in occupation for those who had so long depended on shipbuilding for their livelihood. The latter reason also put boatbuilders throughout Newfoundland out of work, leaving little similar work available in the area.

The caribou herd had returned to a safe level for controlled hunting, following its near extermination by lynx in the early 1920s; and the moose had multiplied to an acceptable hunting population. The government, in a effort to provide work for the unemployed—and to bring much needed outside cash into the province—began an advertising campaign in Canadian and United States sport magazines to promote guiding for moose and caribou hunts. Jack Farrell of North Bay was one of the outfitters listed.

As a result, directly or indirectly, of the promotional program, Jack Farrell, with his cousin Arthur Farrell and Percy Taylor, built up a reasonable number of clients and conducted eight parties to the highlands in at least one year of their guiding.

Henry Schaefer, a writer, was a member of one of those parties. He wrote an article titled "Ox Hunt for Moose" that was published with a series of pictures in the September 1964 issue of *Outdoor Life* magazine. The well-written piece describes the conditions of the moose hunt at that time, and repeating the first part will provide the reader firsthand observations. It follows:

Jack Farrell with Percy Taylor with packsacks on oxen.

We were a strange looking caravan slogging across the Newfoundland muskeg, a queer mixture of modern and ancient, part machined, part on foot. I doubt if anybody would have figured us for what we were, a party of moose hunters with ten miles to go to camp across road-less bogs and up and down rough, boulder strewn hills.

Up ahead, our outfitter, Jack Farrell, chugged along on a weasel, a tractor with tank-like treads designed to travel wet muskeg. Jack was towing a high-bodied, bare-ground sleigh heaped with supplies and equipment. Behind the sleigh, two big, patient pack oxen plodded along under mountainous loads of duffel and gear. Bringing up the rear, the six of us and our two guides trudged after the oxen, trying to pick the driest route across the bog.

This was to be a moose hunt of a special kind. We were in country about as difficult of access as you could find anywhere in the eastern half of Canada. The weasel and oxen were along because they were the only means by which we could trans-

Jack Farrell hauling wood with Bombardier tractor.

port our gear. It takes a jet about two hours to fly from New York City, just across the Hudson River from our homes in New Jersey, to Newfoundland, yet we'd found it necessary to turn back to something as primitive as ox travel.

I had killed ten moose in the 30-odd years I'd been hunting, all of them in Newfoundland, plus six caribou in that same province. As outdoor writer for the *Newark News* since 1947, I've gotten around the continent and taken my share of trophy game—88 animals in all—but I never made a trip quite like this one.

Coming home from a Newfoundland hunt in the fall of 1961 on the motor ship that ferries people and automobiles between the island and the mainland, I had struck up an acquaintance with Bill Bickel, a retired policeman from Paterson, New Jersey. In his early 60s, Bill told me that this had been his sixteenth moose hunt. His first eleven had been in Quebec and the last five in Newfoundland.

He was with a party of seven. All had filled their moose

licenses, and there were some fine heads in the lot. Bickel's story of the road-less country where they had hunted, the pack oxen they used to get into it, and the number of moose they had seen fascinated me. He explained that each year he got together six partners to make the trip with him, and I put in my bid. In the fall of 1963, Bill got in touch with me, and I completed my plans.

The other five in our party were Mike Guilliano, Gus Windeler, Al Sharry, Fred Krug, and Len Kuiken all from New Jersey. They were all in their 40s or 50s and all experienced; they proved to be a fine bunch.

We left home Tuesday, October 8, driving Windeler's half-ton truck and Sharry's station wagon. Both were crammed. Bickel rode with Gus, the rest with Al. We had duffel bags, rifles, cameras, and other gear, and were taking groceries for a week in camp. Bickel knew that the tiny general store at North Bay, where we'd head into the brush, could not supply our needs.

It took three days to drive the 1200 miles to North Sydney, Nova Scotia, with stop-overs in Maine and New Brunswick. We arrived Thursday evening, in fog and rain, and headed for the dock to load our two vehicles aboard the William Carson, a big ferry carrying passengers and cars. It makes a daily trip to Newfoundland and back, seven hours each way. The round-trip fare is $29 for a car, $9 a person, and a sleeping berth cost $2 and up. The ship was close to a hunter's special that rainy night.

We docked at 7 a.m. at Port aux Basques, a picturesque town of less then 5000 built on steep hills overlooking the sea, and drove through without stopping. Most non-resident hunters going to Newfoundland buy their moose licenses ($35 up this year, now $75) from the purser on the Carson, but Bickel had arranged to get ours from the outfitter.

The 433,000 square miles of Newfoundland are largely wilderness, and the southern half is almost totally road-less being composed of lakes and ponds, streams and bogs, hills and low mountains. That was the area where we were headed, in the foothills of the Long Range mountains. Just out of Port aux Basques we turned east on a dirt road that skirted the wild coastline for about thirty miles to the hamlet of Rose Blanche and ended.

Arthur Farrell and Percy Taylor, our guides, were waiting at the dock there with Farrell's twenty-five-foot boat that we'd use for the next leg of our trip, the thirty miles to North Bay. We transferred our gear and shoved off with Art at the wheel and the rest of us crowded into the small cabin, huddled around a smoky wood-burning stove.

The two guides looked like the kind who'd give us a good hunt, and they proved to be just that. Both were native Newfies, close to forty-five, sturdy and weather-beaten. Arthur was Jack Farrell's cousin. It was late afternoon, and raining once more, when we reached North Bay, a cluster of twelve houses tucked under a 1000-foot slope near the head of La Poile Bay, a long arm of the sea that cuts into the rugged coast like a fjord. There was no dock, but Jack Farrell came out in a rowboat to ferry us ashore.

I liked the outfitter's looks. Quick and pleasant, thirty-seven years old, he's been in business twelve years, taking half a dozen parties back into the bush each fall. Moose season opened September 16 last year and ran until December 31, but Farrell takes no hunters after the end of October because of bad weather. When he isn't handling hunters, he builds boats, as do all the men of North Bay.

I had never seen a more interesting place, the houses clean and white, not a car or a horse in the village, and the streets hardly more than footpaths. The houses are heated with wood-burning stoves, there is no running water, and the plumbing is the outside variety. But whatever the village may lack in modern conveniences, it makes up for in friendliness and hospitality. The seven of us were taken to private homes that night. and our welcome couldn't have been warmer.

Early Saturday morning, we packed Farrell's sleigh, put wooden pack-saddles on the two oxen, loaded them, and started the long trudge to camp.

Jack Farrell with ox, Bucko, Andrew Strickland, Gordon and Melvin Farrell in background.

Schaefer's article continued, describing in detail an interesting and successful hunt with a moose for each of the seven hunters, the butchered meat hauled back to the village daily for cutting and packing in cloth bags. He had high praise for Jack and Arthur Farrell and for Percy Taylor.

The inconvenience of the extra days required to get to North Bay and back to Port aux Basques and the strenuous hike to the high-ground hunting camp discouraged all but the most hardy. North Bay sport guiding for moose and caribou could not compete with modern lodges in more accessible areas of Newfoundland and Quebec. And it could provide work for only six weeks of the year for the native guides. They had to find work elsewhere, and left North Bay.

24

Village Reincarnation

Following the gradual exodus of the residents of North Bay, ending when Ernest Farrell was the last to leave, there was little activity there for several years except for the passing through each summer of up to six weekly fishing parties on their way to and from the camp at Salmon Hole. Members of the parties often spent a night or more, when the weather dictated and the river was unsafe or too high to cross, in the big house built by Frank Strickland sixty years earlier. It was the second house built at North Bay. The sagging kitchen ell was removed during the late 1980s but the main house was the last of the original pioneer homes to be demolished.

As the residents of the bay left, they sold the big houses to buyers from La Poile, Petites, Rose Blanche, and other nearby villages who tore them down, salvaged the pit-sawed boards and other reusable materials, transported them in their boats to where they lived, and used them to build or enlarge homes, boathouses, woodsheds or storage sheds.

But the families who had grown up at North Bay had deep ties to their ancestral homeland. Gravestones in a small plot, surrounded by a white picket fence, identify the last resting places of Andrew Strickland and of his mother, Fannie Morris. Also there are the stones of Josiah Farrell and his wife, Julia (Stone), and their two sons, ages twenty and twenty-four and George A. Taylor and his wife, Hannah (Neil), and Barbara Loraine, infant daughter of Mildred and Arthur Farrell. There is a second cemetery at Jimmy's Place, an esker a mile or so down the west side of the bay; and a few bodies lie buried in small plots across the bay

Cemetery plot at North Bay.

Stone of Andrew Strickland.

Stone of George Taylor.

where the Taylor's lived when they first moved to North Bay.

Like the salmon and the trout that return from far away to the river of their ancestors, so too have the descendants of the pioneers of North Bay returned to the land of their fathers. Ernest Farrell purchased the schoolhouse and transformed it into a neat and comfortable cottage. Max and Hilda Strickland built close to the last resting place of his grandfather Andrew. Others returned to build family cottages for summer visits, not necessarily in the following order: Percy and Violet Taylor; Jack and Jane Farrell; Arthur with daughter Verna; three sons of Max and Hilda—Jimmy (staying in Max's cottage,) Andrew, and Norman—with their sister wives Bertha, Gladys, and Myrtle (Stagg). William Farrell built his cottage where Edward's house had stood, across and near the mouth of Drinking Brook. Alec Chant, head guide for Duncan Smith and later for Scott Smith, and his wife, Eilene (Bond), built in the afternoon shadow of Frank Strickland's home, sold later to Frederick Strickland and then purchased by Duncan Smith. (Duncan's son Scott replaced it with a new cottage in 1995.) Tom Farrell, youngest son of Eugene and Mary (Taylor) Farrell, and his wife, Maud (sister of Alec Chant), built their cottage across the river and on the bay. After taking over the position of River Guardian following Max Strickland's retirement, Phil Bond, brother of Eilene Chant (and current River Guardian), and his wife built their cottage on Crown land on the east side of Drinking Brook below the high bank in which the vegetable cellars had been dug, close to the spot where once stood one of the workshops in which boats were built before the 1953 fire.

The lynx that had nearly exterminated the caribou and on occasion killed some of the pastured sheep in the early years of the settlement were now seldom seen; however, black bears now became visitors to the village as well as to the hunting and fishing camps on the mountains and up river. On one occasion in the early 1970s a bear made a nocturnal visit to one of the houses. He climbed the porch roof, made his entrance through a second-story window, and proceeded to examine most of the rooms before departing through a ground-floor window. Another time when Ernest Farrell was sleeping in his comfortable cottage

Stone of Josiah Farrell.

Stone of Barbara Loraine Farrell.

(originally the village schoolhouse), a bear woke him while attempting to enter through the front door. Hearing Ernest scrambling to determine the cause of the racket, the bear left, only to find and dig into Max Strickland's garbage pail. Max guessed the cause of the noise and came out with a loaded rifle. He shot three times as the bear retreated into the darkness. There may have been a family of bears that came to the village that night: Morning revealed that three of the then empty houses had been visited, causing considerable damage. Moose frequently wander within sight of the village and an early riser may peer from his window to see a curious moose just outside.

The sounds of lawn mowers and gas-powered electric generators have replaced those once made by hammers, hand saws, and planes. Voices echo above the constant ring of the river flowing over rocks and from the falls of Drinking Water Brook as children play Frisbee on the neatly mowed lawns where their parents and grandparents as children themselves brought water in buckets from the brook and chips in baskets from the boat shops through the grass-lined paths to the houses.

We can never know how the pioneers of North Bay envisioned their future or that of their children. But they were well aware that great changes would take place and in which they would take part. Andrew Strickland first saw the economic possibilities of the natural resources of the La Poile River valley. He convinced Thomas Farrell to stake his future and that of his family on moving there; and Andrew remained there during his lifetime to support and promote the village he and his brother Frank had founded. Josiah Farrell the inventor, used his imagination and talents to reduce the menial, manual labor requirements of constructing boats; and with his work ethic, jovial nature, and religious convictions, may have been a "big frog in a little puddle," but those characteristics under any other circumstances would have made him a leader of men.

Frank Strickland and, near the same time, Minnie Farrell (1930) were the first to leave the village, taking their capabilities and their expectations to the United States and to Ontario and to spread their seeds in a wider world, both proud of their ancestry and of the country and circumstances of their birth.

25

A New North Bay

By 1965 Duncan Smith and farm machinery dealer Ron Baltzer had joined the Kentville fishing party; Carl Ross, a retired Canadian Air Force pilot, joined the group in 1967. All were from Nova Scotia. Duncan Smith was born in Unionville, Ontario. He completed his veterinary degree in 1952, and in partnership with a classmate opened a veterinary clinic in Kentville the following year. Duncan married in 1954 and he and his wife, Alice, raised three sons and a daughter.

Duncan was a tall man, six feet four inches, with broad shoulders, a light complexion, and a genial nature. He was always willing to do more than his share of whatever was necessary to make a hunting or fishing trip successful for other party members. He had made several hunting trips to North Bay with the Dr. Schaffner party before 1965, but not on an annual basis, and not both hunting and fishing the same year.

The last boat, a sixty-foot long-liner, was completed in the boathouse at North Bay before 1967. Lack of work and pressures from the government for the villagers to accept a financial incentive to leave, caused the population to dwindle to but a few of the older inhabitants. Six of the original houses stood deserted and empty.

Frederick Strickland was one of those who stayed on. He and Percy Taylor guided the Kentville hunting party for the last time. Three oxen carried the supplies in saddlebags. One of the animals, with his pawing and "moaning" kept the party awake a good part of the night in the log cabin at Salmon Hole. Dr. Foley probably correctly surmised that the animal had not been completely castrated—that one testicle had not dropped before the procedure, and thus the animal was still a bull. Needless to say, the animal was not taken to the hunting camp on the high land.

Caribou and moose were plentiful that year and Duncan Smith was a lucky hunter. He accounted for three of the caribou shot by the party. When Dr. Schaffner, handicapped by being unable to see anything in a narrow slit straight ahead, had not got his moose, Dunc went with him, located a trophy specimen, and got the doctor close enough for a good shot. Schaffner was still unable to get the animal in his sights. When the moose became wary and started to bolt, Dunc accurately fired the necessary shot.

Returning from the hunt, Frederick Strickland informed the party that he was leaving the bay and would not be available for guiding the following season. His house and land were for sale. Duncan Smith, considering the convenience to parties coming to hunt or fish of having an abode there, such as had always been available for an overnight stay going and coming between La Poile and Salmon Hole, bought the property and its contents and the log cabin at Salmon Hole. A receipt in full was dated October 1967. Within a few years, all but three of the original houses were torn down, with the Frederick Strickland house dominating the village area.

The abandonment of the village as a year-round habitation triggered a series of changes. With Frederick gone, there would be the need for a replacement guide. Tom Farrell, from Rose Blanche, with Alec Chant, his brother-in-law from La Poile as assistant, were hired in 1969. Max Strickland, son of Frederick, had moved to Petites in 1966 but returned to the village in summer and retained his job as River Guardian (warden). Gradually, small cottages replaced the old houses as previous residents returned and spent vacations and even some whole summers at North Bay.

A caterpillar-tread Bombardier replaced some of the oxen and was used for several years (until its owner moved away) to transport firewood to the village and supplies for the fishermen at the Salmon Hole camp.

The spring fishing party of 1972 from Kentville consisted of Dr.

Schaffner, Carl Ross, Ian Baird, Dr. Foley, Duncan Smith, and Dunc's thirteen-year-old son, Scott. They were met at Rose Blanche by Alec Chant, brother-in-law of head guide Tom Farrell, in Tom's twenty-six-foot-long fishing boat. The weather was normal for Newfoundland at that season; thick fog, showers, and windy with a rough sea, but nothing that Alec and the fishing boat had not experienced many times.

Young Scott promptly became seasick and spent the two-and-a-half-hour trip near the rail, paying attention to little beyond his own problems. Carl Ross rested on the bags of supplies and equipment in the cabin, and Alec was at the wheel as the boat progressed easterly inside coastal islands, where the waves and wind were somewhat subdued compared to those in the open sea. The rest of the party were on the open deck, feeling less susceptible to seasickness in the open air. They kept an eye on young Scott, or perhaps they just wanted to be closer to the rail should they be overcome by the boat's movements.

Dr. Schaffner was passing through the cabin door when the boat, in a narrow area between a wave-pounded island ledge on one side and a low mainland cliff on the other, was struck by a twisting current and jolted suddenly to one side. The doctor lost his balance, grabbed the door jamb, and was swung around. He hit his head a severe bump on a post in the cabin. He sat down beside Carl but soon complained of a headache. He got up and went out on the deck. As they approached La Poile, Dunc Smith came into the cabin and asked Carl what was wrong with Schaffner, that he seemed incoherent. They helped the doctor into the cabin and he rested in the spot where Carl had been. His condition deteriorated, however, and by the time they docked in La Poile, he was unconscious.

Dr. Foley correctly diagnosed a hemorrhage inside the skull that was exerting pressure on the brain. Carl, a member of the Canadian Air Rescue Team, phoned the emergency connection, but due to the foggy conditions, planes and helicopters were grounded. He was able to arrange with the Royal Canadian Mounted Police at Port aux Basques to meet them at Rose Blanche and for a plane to be waiting at Stephenville to take

Schaffner to a hospital in Nova Scotia. Carl, Dr. Foley, and Alec returned to Rose Blanche with the unconscious Schaffner as quickly as possible and were met by the RCMP, who took them at high speed to the airport. Dr. Schaffner died on the plane before it could reach the hospital. The plane, without authority to transport a corpse, returned to Summerside and the RCMP and members of the fishing party returned to Stephenville.

Carl Ross and Dr. Foley remained overnight at Port aux Basques and made the necessary phone calls before returning to La Poile. Dr. Schaffner was in his mid-seventies and had often said that he wanted to die while fishing on the La Poile. He came close to achieving that destiny.

Tom Farrell led the solemn party on the three-mile trek, wading the river near the bay, over the rocks and through the neglected hay fields, between the grotesque giant yellow birches, wading the river again where it split a half mile from the cabin, all carrying heavy packs as well as their rods. No oxen were left at North Bay, and the owner of the Bombardier had scrapped it behind the boat shed at North Bay. There was no other way to get their food and supplies to the cabin other than packing everything on their backs. It was just as well that their time at Salmon Hole camp was shortened by the tragedy. Without doubt, during the evening hours, after the day's salmon catch had been canned, sealed, and preserved in the steam pressure cooker, there was many a glass raised around the table in the hissing, bright light of the Coleman gas lamp in memory of Dr. Verne Schaffner.

26

Transition

Like Dr. Verne Schaffner, his friend and salmon fishing mentor, Duncan Smith had developed a deep and lasting attachment to North Bay, the La Poile River, and the old log cabin at Salmon Hole pool. Now, as owner of Frederick Strickland's property at North Bay and of the old log cabin at Salmon Hole, Dunc accepted the responsibilities of "party manager" of the Kentville salmon fishermen, an "office" he had probably already been serving for the aging doctor. He also recognized that in order to maintain dominance and retain the privacy of the river, it would be necessary to support guides for the season by expanding occupancy of the cabin by fishermen for the full six-week season.

Dunc visited Dr. Schaffner's widow and family and confirmed his intent to carry on the annual Newfoundland fishing trips. From acquaintances made in local organizations of which he was a member, friends from veterinary college, and members of the professional organizations to which he belonged, Dunc gradually filled party after party to participate in fishing on the La Poile.

He built, or had built by the guides, a bunkhouse addition to the back of the old log cabin that could sleep six, leaving the original cabin space available for a wood cookstove, a sink, and a dinner (and card-playing) table. The old cookhouse was torn down and a suitable bunkhouse built for the guides. Without oxen to transport food and supplies to the mountain lean-to camps, the hunting trips were discontinued.

With the end of permanent residents at North Bay and the scrapping of the Bombardier with caterpillar treads, Dunc, in the early 1970s, purchased an old King farm tractor from Ron Baltzer, a Kentville-area farm equipment dealer and fishing party member. It was shipped to La Poile, loaded onto a platform over two small boats, and towed on a fair day with a smooth sea to North Bay. Ron Baltzer built a trailer that was similarly transported to North Bay. The combination provided a way to get the food, fishing rods, and other material upriver. Carl Ross taught Alec Chant, by then established as head guide for Dunc's parties, to drive the "monster." Alec, always having lived at La Poile, where there were no roads or automobiles, never had need to learn to drive. Once at the steering wheel of the monster, it is doubtful that any previous experience on normal highways would have been any advantage in learning to maneuver the old tractor over the river rocks.

Dunc Smith paid little attention to frills for his guests or partners on the fishing trips. The roughly built cabin continued to exist without improvements, the board bunks without mattresses, and the outhouse slightly tipped. The iron cookstove got a new stovepipe only when the old one rusted through or was crushed by a visiting bear. Dunc brought vegetables from his own garden to help keep the cost of food as low as possible and participated in catching a few cod down near the East Bay junction to supplement the diet. And he passed the savings on to his fellow fishermen.

On at least one occasion, Carl and Dr. Grant Worthylake, another Kentville party member, accompanied Alec during a stopover at North Bay to return to the cod fishing area four miles down the bay in a small rowboat powered by an old extended shaft outboard motor. They had hardly started jigging when the water near them appeared to rise several feet and "boil." Alec recognized the presence of a large whale and acted quickly to start the motor and exit the area. In his hurry to get the boat in motion, he jammed the motor into gear with the engine at high starting speed. The drive shaft broke, and they were left without power a long distance from the village. Alec, alert to the possibility of motor failure, had whittled out fresh "Newfy" oarlocks; that is, oarlocks made of slippery green alder from which the oars frequently escaped. With the tide nearing high, they started the long row back, getting only about halfway before the tide turned,

Max Strickland and Ernest Farrell, grandsons of pioneers.

Max drawing logs into saw mill building.

adding to their labor and misery.

Bears had always been a problem at the Salmon Hole cabin. Back when Percy Taylor was assisting Frederick Strickland in guiding fishermen, Percy had lined the guides camp window with fishhooks in an attempt to discourage bears from entering. Now, as the party approached the cabin on their annual trip, they noticed the iron bars twisted off the window, and the glass and frame not carefully removed. The cabin door bore deep scratches from the claws of the intruder, who had broken the hinges in leaving. The oven door of the woodstove hung by one twisted hinge; the other was broken off as a result of the bear's displeasure at not finding the food he expected.

Carl Ross vividly remembers waking one night at the old log cabin as the door appeared to explode. Thinking it must have been a gust of wind, he got up, pulled the door closed, and hooked it. Telling the experience at the table the next morning, he was reminded there had been no wind during the night. A daylight look at the outside of the door revealed new deep claw marks left by the would-be visitor. The fishermen agreed that the

Rollers used to make logs draw easier.

Ernest Farrell patching roof on saw mill building.

bear may have found the inside smell offensive, causing his retreat.

Ernest Farrell, with his brother-in-law James Strickland, occasionally returned to North Bay from Cobourg, Ontario, where they had settled after leaving North Bay. In 1978 Ernest "retired" and began spending each summer at North Bay. He reactivated the old half-ton, single-cylinder engine that powered the sawmill and with help from Max Strickland, they started sawing boards and dimension timbers. But this time, rather than to build boats, the lumber was used to rebuild the village. They sawed the lumber to construct a cottage for Max, one for Percy Taylor, and another for Max's son Norman.

Within a few years, the village was rebuilt with cozy cottages that replaced the multi-roomed two story homes of the original pioneers. Only the big house of Frederick Strickland, before that his uncle Frank's, the second house built at North Bay and now the property of Duncan Smith, remained. Gradually it lost its porch up to the kitchen door, then the kitchen ell, a giant, grotesque monster left among the increasing number of small

"Now it's a lonely lovely place where wildlife runs riot and the few houses, one being our original home and another our grandfather's home, still stand, looking lost and lonely among the trees and flowers that are run wild," wrote Pearl Farrell, daughter of Josiah.
Original buildings in 1981.

"summer" cottages. And once again the sounds of children playing returned to North Bay, the sounds of children of a later generation of the original pioneers, along with the children of the men who guided the fishing parties from Nova Scotia, who had been guided by Frederick Strickland and Edward Farrell, their friends, and their sons.

27

Author's Diary

When Dick Goodell and I arrived at my camp in eastern Maine late in the evening on June 25, 1980, it seemed as if we had waited forever to start on our first Atlantic salmon fishing trip to Newfoundland. In fact, Dr. Duncan Smith, a long time business acquaintance and friend, had invited me when we met at the New Hampshire Poultry Health Conference on April 3. Dunc, as the genial six-foot four-inch veterinarian was called, had also agreed that there would be room for our mutual friend Dick Goodell, for a fee. Dick would be a welcome companion for me on the long drive from New Hampshire to our meeting place in Sydney, Nova Scotia.

Now we had driven 258 miles on the first leg of the trip. My diary records that because of the exceptionally warm weather, which promoted a horde of blackflies and mosquitoes that permeated the hunting-fishing camp, we did not sleep well, if at all, that night. I wonder, however, if the expectations of our first Atlantic salmon fishing trip were not an equal cause of our insomnia.

According to my diary, we rose early the next morning and had a camp breakfast of bacon, eggs, toast, and coffee. We loaded my pickup truck with clothes and gear and passed through the customs at St. Stephen, New Brunswick, well before the rush-hour traffic. Including time for lunch at the Bluebird Restaurant in Sussex, a stop to refill the fuel tank, and one to be welcomed to Nova Scotia by a kilted bagpipe player at Amherst, we drove five hundred miles in eleven hours and arrived at the ferry parking lot at North Sydney at seven p.m. Dunc Smith arrived an hour

Guides and gear in one cylinder in-board motor boat transporting sports' gear to North Bay from LaPoile.

later with Dr. Horace Foley (Doc) and Carl Ross, and we boarded the huge oceangoing ferry for the hundred-mile crossing to Port aux Basques. Dunc slept in his sleeping bag on the floor of the four-bunk stateroom during the overnight crossing.

We continued our transportation by ferry on the coastal Runner, a transformed Canadian wartime one-hundred-foot PT boat, more than forty miles along the south eastern shoreline to where a headland marked the entrance to La Poile harbor. There, on the wharf, our guides took charge. Head guide Alec Chant sent us along the steep gravel path to his house on the rock hill at the edge of the village, where his wife, Eilene, served us tea and cake while he and guides Reggie Chant (not related) and Lewis Bond stowed supplies and equipment into an open, single-cylinder-powered seventeen foot motorboat. By the time we returned to the dock, Reggie and Lewis had wrapped their cargo in a colorful tarp. We joined them in a second, similar boat and were on our way around the headland and into the mouth of North Bay for the nine-mile, two-hour trip to the head of the bay and mouth of the La Poile River.

Guide Lewis Bond nets a cod for Carl Ross.

The landing at North Bay.

Two miles or more into the trip, where the bay widened, Alec stopped the engine and we jigged for cod to supplement the camp food supply. Carl hooked a big one, and after much effort with an undersized rod and reel, brought it to the surface and Lewis netted the thirty-five-pound cod, then we were again on our way. Escorted by several low-flying black-back gulls hopeful of a handout, and scrutinized from time to time by bald eagles and ospreys soaring high above, we chugged steadily through the wide area where East Bay enters and onward between the increasingly higher mountains and resulting narrower bay. We listened to the "old-friends" talk among guide Alec, Dunc, Carl, and Doc, about salmon and salmon pools and a bear that had broken into the camp and torn the oven door from the cookstove. They discussed flies, Green Butts, Cosseboom, Thunder and Lightning, and Dunc displayed a batch of large, fluffy, White Wulff dry flies, his favorite even in early season.

The boats were beached on the shore, not sand, but waterworn small, black, slatelike rocks. Several boathouses fronted back from the beach, and a half-dozen houses situated in a small field beyond a ten-foot-high riverbank made up the village. Dunc had purchased a two story house from one of the original residents of the village. We had dinner there, prepared by one of the guides, while the other guides transferred our supplies and gear to a trailer hitched behind an ancient King tractor. We crossed the brackish water where the river meets the bay, challenging the height of our hip boots. We followed the tractor and trailer over an unmarked trail on the river-rounded rocks and between ice-scarred fir and yellow birch two miles on the split river island, stopping occasionally at a pool to cast a fly. Then again we challenged the swift river to cross where the river had split. From there it was a short mile to the high bank above Salmon Hole Pool and the old log cabin. Dunc had previously added a bunk room to the back of the cabin and on this trip had brought four-inch foam mattresses to soften the board springs. There was a small building nearby with bunks for the guides and an electric freezer. They had brought in a portable electric generator, which, set up outside, provided power for the freezer and for a few bulbs in the cabin.

View up river from North Bay village.

The next morning Dunc took Dick and me to Dunc's Pool, a short way below where we had crossed the river on our way up. He went to great pains to explain and demonstrate his very successful method of fly-fishing for Atlantic salmon. In the process, and following us through the pool, he caught two salmon while we learned lessons we would never forget...and missed hooking several fish that were attracted to our flies.

At noon back at the camp for lunch, I noticed that one of my boots had filled with water from a leak by the heel that could not be repaired. I had purchased them in Calais, not realizing they were made for clam-diggers wading in mud. They were heavy and stiff—most unsuitable for sportfishing on rocks in fast water. Alec loaned me his boots for the remainder of the trip, for which I was most grateful. Before the day was over, Carl caught a sea trout (actually, an arctic char) of about four pounds, a beautiful fish.

I shall never forget the pool, the details, or the experience of the next afternoon, June 29, 1980. Dunc and the guides had taken us along the shaded path through the woods in back of camp past Lower Salmon Pool, over the huge rocks that sheltered Salmon

Tractor fords the LaPoile river with gear and supplies.

Hole Brook and along the steep and treacherous ledges beside Upper Salmon Pool. I missed a good strike at Foley's Pool, but both Dunc and Dick hooked and netted salmon there. We went on several miles to Doctor's Pool, where we ate lunch that the guides had brought; but caught no fish there. On the return trip, Dunc caught a salmon in a pool above Foley's. Back at Upper Salmon Pool, Lewis and Reggie stationed me on a rock outcrop from the steep ledge bank about half way of the pool. From their position on the ledge, they could look into the water and see several salmon and were trying to help me position my casts for the proper approach: "A little longer cast." "Too far beyond." "Make the fly swing toward me." "You're getting close." Although I could not seem to place the fly correctly, a salmon they had not seen suddenly rose and took my fly. He streaked the length of the pool, the reel screaming, the line into the backing. He went to the bottom of the deepest part of the pool and sulked for several minutes while I, shaking like a leaf, attempted to regain composure. There was help from the guides, verbal: "Keep your rod tip up." "Don't let that line get loose." "Drop the rod tip when he jumps."

That salmon was an acrobat. He was in the water, out of it, and

The rocky trail to Salmon Hole camp.

A rocky crossing half a mile from camp.

back in again. He came straight for me and made abrupt turns as if to climb the rocks on either side. My line was loose, my rod tip down. Reeled almost to the net, he skipped across the surface of the pool in leaps and bounds again and again. It was all over in a minute, or was it an hour? When Lewis finally netted that six-pound fish, I had no idea how long it had been since he took the fly. I stood in a cold sweat, trembling and unsteady on the rock. Lewis grabbed my arm, afraid I was about to fall into the river. I think I was.

Dunc and Dick partway down from Doctor's Pool had crossed the river and fished down on the other side. They arrived in time to witness the final minutes of the fray. Resting, I sat beside Dunc on a shelf of the steep ledge and in all sincerity confided that I as well as the salmon had just been hooked, hooked on Atlantic salmon fishing and on the La Poile River in Newfoundland. And I asked what he could do about it. Dunc laughed, obviously pleased that I had caught a salmon. He admitted to an ulterior motive in inviting me. He told me some of his La Poile fishing partners had grown too old to make the trip, and in considering

Original log cabin in 1980.

Host Duncan Smith with Dr. Foley.

acquaintances who might be a reliable source to bring a party of fishermen to his camp, he had thought of me. Then he asked if I would be interested in bringing a six-fisherman party each year to fill a scheduled week. With four sons brought up with summer weekends of camping and fishing trout streams of the White Mountains of New Hampshire and the wilderness streams of Thoreau's Maine, I did not hesitate.

During the rest of the week, in spite of a rainstorm that raised the river temporarily by ten feet, I caught two more salmon. Our party filled the possession limit of twenty-four fish, several of which were arctic char of four to six pounds. I might have caught more fish myself had I not been so fascinated with the grandeur of the mountains, the beautiful river, the wildflowers, the rocks, and the moose—even the mink that tried to steal a salmon from me that I had hidden under a heavy rock to save from a scavenging seagull.

Atlantic Salmon

With rod in hand, boots in the stream,
My fly is cast again, again....
Not always where I thought it would,
Or leader tangled into knots.
But patience then, untangle them
And start with shorter line.
Too long it seems before a strike;
Sit on the bank and change the fly,
Then cast some more, change back again.
No luck today and day near end
With aching arm, cold tired feet,
About to quit, go back to camp;
And then the line is pulled away
Through fingers numb with wet and cold.
The reel alive and screaming now,
Unwinding line upon demand.
The rod tip up, instinctive now,
To power surge at end of line
And bend of rod to equalize.
The battle's on. Forgotten now
The tangled line, the aching arm.
The salmon jumps completely out
And splashes back, is off again,
Swims up the stream and deep below
And bends the line at waters edge.
If caught or not, it's here and now
This day was spent to talk about,
Relive in dreams, hope to repeat,
And keep always in memory.

Walter Staples

28

"The King is dead: long live the King"

The morning of November 10, 1983, Duncan Smith's wife, Alice, had completed breakfast preparations but Dunc did not come to the table. Hearing no sounds from the bedroom, she went back to call him, but Dunc's heart had stopped beating, and he had died peacefully in his sleep. At age fifty-five, veterinarian, Duncan Smith, husband, father of three sons and a daughter, was dead.

When he died, the fishing pleasures he had enjoyed with friends over a period of twenty years, his leadership and determination to continue life of North Bay ended. But the result of his efforts was an organization that would help maintain the life of this small and remote Newfoundland village.

Frederick Strickland's big house served as a reminder of their pioneer background to those who had been born and had grown up at North Bay. It brought them back to build cottages nearby in which to spend summers with their children, some of them the fourth and fifth generations of the original pioneers. Dunc's development of the weekly fishing parties required transportation to and from La Poile on a regular weekly schedule. It provided a transportation safety net as well as a scheduled "ferry" service without charge for many relatives and friends, who often took advantage by riding to or from North Bay from La Poile as they visited their cottages. And food and fuel were freely carried back and forth as a neighborly service. The established weekly fishing parties provided summer employment for three guides for six weeks, and eventually additional weeks before and after the season were spent making camp and equipment improve-

Dunc Smith

Last of original buildings at North Bay in 1981.

ments. The fishermen from Nova Scotia, other parts of Canada, and from the United States brought additional money to the area by way of costs for licenses, flies, food, and transportation. And as Dunc had, they brought friendship as well.

The presence of fishermen on the river meant the need for a government River Guardian. This position was filled by a local individual.

Perhaps most important, by continuing the seasonal guiding activity that had long been part of the survival of North Bay, the village had a reason to survive, at least during the summer.

Many changes took place over the years when Duncan Smith made his hunting and fishing pilgrimages to North Bay. The last long-liner was built. The residents were essentially forced to move away from their ancestral homes and their work. All of the original two-story homes were torn down, with the exception of the one Dunc had purchased. Many of the original residents and members of their families built small cottages, to which they returned for all or part of each summer. These cottages were, by cooperating efforts, provided with running water piped from Drinking Brook, and electricity from portable gasoline generators. Radios provided contact with fishermen at sea and families at La Poile and other nearby villages.

With fond memories of old friends and hunting and fishing experiences, Dunc preferred not to make many changes in the old log cabin even though the rotting lower logs each year left the roof nearer the floor. A fisherman was more likely to bump his head when going through the door. Dunc eventually purchased a small generator that would support one bulb in the cabin. He ran it occasionally during the day to operate a freezer in which to keep fish rather than pressure cook and can those caught by party members. And he brought in foam mattresses to make the rough, board bunks more comfortable.

Though generally the La Poile is a friendly river during fishing season, bark scrapes as high as ten feet on the trunks of the huge

Inside the old log cabin.

Scott Smith (far right) at old log cabin 1980.

yellow birches are witness to the power of huge ice cakes riding roaring floods across the valley floor between the two river branches. One year Max Strickland was needed to come in a high-powered outboard following a hurricane to rescue the fishermen from Salmon Hole camp when the river reached a dangerous level.

In Carl Ross's words, "The rain started at about two in the afternoon and by midnight the river was up by at least fifteen feet. It looked like a two- or three-day wait to get out; so Dunc and I walked up to Salmon Hole Brook. It was impressive. As we viewed the scenery, Max Strickland and his wife, Hilda, arrived in a boat powered by two outboard motors, forty horsepower and twenty-five horsepower. They picked us off a rock at Salmon Hole Brook and stopped at Salmon Hole camp for the rest of the party; and we made one very rapid trip to North Bay, seeing the occasional alder tip sticking out of the water. A memorable trip by any standard."

During the late 1970s, during the spring ice out, an ice dam at the point where the river divides to east and west sides of the valley blocked the east side and forced the entire flow to follow the west side down to the bay. The great power of the flow resulted in new channels and changed pools, and what had been the main river flow on the east side, with the salmon holding pools, was transferred to the west side which then became the major route of the incoming salmon.

With Dunc's unexpected passing, the family asked Carl Ross temporarily to carry on the task of confirming availability of guides, contacting the fishermen, booking the parties, and making the financial and other many arrangements necessary to maintain continuity of the angling parties to La Poile, North Bay, and on to Salmon Hole.

The King was dead, but his son, Scott, who now owned the old house at North Bay and the cabin by Salmon Hole Pool, would be another king to keep alive the action and the spirit of the La Poile River salmon fishermen.

The King was dead, but the pattern was set. Like an oasis in the desert, the village of North Bay would remain, if no more than a private summer resort and an overnight rest and safety stop for annual groups of dedicated and loyal salmon fishermen.

29

Under New Management

The unpleasant experiences, seasickness, and the accident causing Dr. Verne Schaffner's death did not prevent Scott Smith from continued interest in making fishing trips to Salmon Hole on the La Poile River. During high school and college and into his years of employment, he made six trips during the eleven years before his father's death in 1983. Like his father, he developed a love of fishing, an appreciation for the natural beauty of the region, and a sincere respect for the local inhabitants. It was only natural that he would take over the North Bay property and the well-organized schedule of parties that Duncan Smith had developed.

Though Scott had enjoyed the fishing and the camaraderie with members of fishing parties and the guides, his plans for the development of the system were not hampered by memories. His father had, in holding to the past, resisted making any changes in the dilapidated facilities at Salmon Hole. But with the change in management, the guides brought their complaints to Scott of the impossibility of maintaining a clean environment in the ancient cabin, of their own crowded sleeping quarters, and of their inability any longer to make a trip up the river without major repairs to, or replacement of, the old King tractor.

Scott recognized Alec Chant, head guide, with his brother Sidney and the unrelated Reginald Chant to be key components of the system, particularly because of his own non-native and seldom present status. Then living in Calgary, and not always able to make the trip each year, Scott was dependent upon Alec and his assistants for complete management of at least six parties annually. Their duties included getting the parties up to the cabin and back, the guiding requirements including cooking, handling any emergencies that might (and do) occur, and treating fishermen in such a way that every member of each party would want to return the following year. Alec, Sid, and Reg proved more than capable of handling their responsibilities.

Scott began a series of improvements. In June 1985, the first salmon fishing party of the season christened a new fishing camp. It was built on posts four feet above the ground to keep out bears and had a comfortable deck on the front overlooking the upper end of Salmon Hole Pool. Six bunks in tiers of two left space for gear and clothes to be stored in the back room. The kitchen had both a wood and a gas stove, counter, and sink (not then with running water), and there was a dining table in the front room. Good light came from side and front windows. Building it the previous fall had provided the guides with several weeks of additional work. The guides built a new bunkhouse for themselves the following year.

Occasionally a visiting helicopter landed on the rocks between Peter's and Allen's Pools. A fisherman or two would cast on those and Foley's Pool for a short period, then take off. It did not happen often enough to be much competition to the Salmon Hole camp fishermen. One day a smaller (Bumblebee) helicopter circled the camp a few times and, with the water low, made a landing on the rocks right in front of camp. They were inspectors from the well-organized Newfoundland Department of Tourism and Oceans: They had finally found the La Poile and its single sporting camp. Members of one or more of the parties, when attending some of the larger fishermen's shows, had visited the Newfoundland booths and enthusiastically mentioned their good fortune to have fished the La Poile. The secret was out.

The government camp inspector for the area, Len Rich, contacted Scott and advised him to register his camp with the Department of Tourism; otherwise, the hosting of salmon anglers would have to stop. The necessary paperwork was completed and a lease was obtained for the land on which the camp was located. Dunc had purchased the house and land at North Bay and the log cabin at Salmon Hole Pool. The land on which the cabin was located was owned by the Crown. With his Tourism permit and Crown land lease in hand, the sportfishing camp on the La Poile River became an "official" Salmon Outfitting Camp. As such, it was necessary for Scott to upgrade and standardize the facilities. In fact, it would be asking no more than Scott was doing and intended to continue; and it also provided protection against anyone else building or operating a similar fishing camp on the La Poile.

Scott authorized improvements, made by the guides, during the following years that included running water in the sink and a flush toilet and shower in a separate outside building. The water was heated on sunny days in the long plastic pipe that brings it—more than two thousand feet—from Salmon Hole Brook down to the camp area.

The old King tractor was replaced with a newer (but also old) Ford tractor. When this became unreliable, a second "backup" Ford tractor was added with a second trailer. A "three-wheeler" is also there for quicker (and rough) rides to and from the village and camp.

Until 1994 the original Frank Strickland house, the last of the original pioneer homes, dominated the rebuilt village at North Bay. It was occasionally used for overnight stops for the parties when the ferries, the tides, or the river water level made such a delay necessary. No longer a safe haven, and then an eyesore in the neat small village, Scott had the guides tear it down and build a neat cottage in its place.

Surprisingly, much of the pit-sawed hand-hewed lumber that made up the frame of the old house, built a hundred years before, was still in good condition. Tony Bond, a resourceful young man from La Poile, and son of longtime guide Lewis Bond, asked Scott for permission to salvage the useful lumber. Though the structure of the pioneer house would disappear, its lumber would take the shape of a new home for the recently married young couple.

After just about one hundred years, the last home of the original village was gone. Only the remains of one of the vegetable storage "cellars" dug in the bank next to the boat workshops remained. And among the weeds and bushes, surrounded by a broken fence in the middle of the village, are the gravestones of Andrew Strickland, his mother Fanny Morris, George Taylor and his wife Hannah (Neil), and Barbara Loraine, infant daughter of Arthur and Mildred Farrell.

30

Budworm and Asides

Neither the guides nor any of the fishermen—not even the grandsons of the original settlers, who had spent most of their lives at North Bay—remembered a spruce budworm infestation in the La Poile River valley. That covered a span of more than eighty years. Though generally referred to as the spruce budworm, the pestilence was even more deadly to fir, and fir trees dominated the tree species in the valley and the mountainsides above North Bay.

The infestation became noticeable during the summer of 1990, when small patches of brown showed on the hillsides. Undoubtedly, though, the moths and the worms that hatched from their eggs had invaded the area several years before, accumulating until they reached the population level that could defoliate and kill the trees. In another year, entire mountainsides had turned brown, the dead spills shedding, leaving the skeletons of trees standing.

The budworms starved from their own predation. Dormant seeds of the fir and spruce came to life and the seedlings of a future forest began to grow in the shade of raspberry bushes and the massive rubble of fallen, dead trees. Through shaded woodland shortcuts between bends in the river where fishermen had trod deep, sometimes muddy, paths between pools, the fallen trees now formed obstacles that had to be removed. These trees were so thick, crisscrossed and held suspended at various levels, that moose no longer came down from the mountains to feed on the buds and leaves of yellow birch and some white maple. The yellow birch, which the moose and caribou had pruned quite thoroughly for many years, now extended center sprouts that

Devastation by spruce budworm infestation.

would someday be logs, out of the reach of moose when the dead tree barriers rotted and the big animals returned.

It is hoped that the roots of the new forest will grow soon enough and be adequate to hold the thin soil on the steep slopes to avoid an increase in the number of ribbonlike slides that mark the mountain walls, so obvious from the bay and river valley, or an avalanche of wider expanse that would narrow the bay or dam the river.

Except for the sparse mature yellow birch and some damaged but surviving spruce, the valley forest is little different from a modern clear-cut, changing the habitat in different and unknown ways from what it long has been.

For a week or more, Alec had quietly watched a wood duck enter stealthily and leave a hole in the side of a fallen tree. One day, as we rested during the midday sun on the camp deck, he pointed to the leaning stump and told us, "They have hatched." He had hardly mentioned it when with the mother duck, flying in circles, called a dozen or more of the tiny black-and-white ducklings to pour from the hole and fall the several feet into the brush and raspberry bushes below. Only their incessant, high-pitched peep-peeps identified their presence in the tangle of the

A days 'keep' for party.

riverbank until they suddenly appeared with their mother in a small river eddy and floated downstream in a tight group.

There was never a salmon caught except under the keen eyesight of a soaring gull that circled patiently while the fish was played, netted, and cleaned. It soared at a safe distance until the lucky fisherman and guide left, then performed the double responsibility of obtaining food and removing the fish entrails from the environment.

Guide Sidney Chant made intermediate use of the fish entrails. He tied them together with fine thread, attached the "blob" to one end of a fish line, threw it into a deep pool, and, when an eel had fastened its curly teeth upon the "morsel," pulled the squirming snake-like fish onto the rocky shore.

We often saw beaver swimming in the deeper river pools. One pair dammed a small stream where it entered the La Poile above the old camp pool and built a substantial lodge around the roots and stump of a large fir tree. By season's end; their pool was teeming with four- to six-inch brook trout that would rise to salmon flies half their own length.

And many a bright July morning, a walk from the camp to a pool downriver was interrupted by frequent stops to harvest and eat wild strawberries along the grassy riverbank.

31

The La Poile River

Water evokes images, from the lack of it in a desert to its expanse in mid-ocean, from a filled glass on the dinner table to a flushing toilet. In its forms as lakes, rivers, springs, and falls, (such as Yosemite, Niagara and Victoria) it inspires poetry and song: "Old Man River," "Red River Valley," "Song of the Chattahoochie." Whatever its natural form, each body of water has its own character, expression, and memories.

The La Poile River—from its beginnings in many springs, and as runoff in small streams from the rock-rubble top of Newfoundland's two thousand foot mountains to its tidewater destination at North Bay—is no exception.

During a warm day in late July, after a week or more without rain, its demure approach to the bay raises hardly more than a murmur as it embraces large stones that deter the central flow or rubs the clean, rounded rocks on each side. Even the falls between the pools are humble and the salmon remain fixed, wide-eyed, grouped side by side in deep water, no more than a tail movement to indicate they are alive. Only at dawn or near sunset will one break the mirror surface of a pool or rise to a fisherman's fly.

Sunshine is brief on the upper river, even during the longest days. The nearer thousand feet and higher peaks on each side shade the morning sun from the east, the evening sun from the west. Midday brings a rising upriver breeze and scudding clouds, reducing blackfly irritation and impeding fly-casting accuracy.

But there are times when the river displays an opposite

Salmon Brook after hurricane rain

extreme. It reacts with a vengeance when the spent wind of an Atlantic hurricane spreads black clouds and a night of torrential rain over the Newfoundland mountains. There is little soil to absorb the rain and the rock-lined lakes overflow, sending the deluge frothing from shelf to shelf, boulder to polished boulder, into the valley a thousand or more feet below. It swells the river, speeds the flow, ten feet higher against the ledge banks, into the struggling alders, crisscrossing the islands on previously dry rock beds, rolling huge rocks, changing the flow in pools. The roar of the falls of Salmon Brook into the Upper Salmon Brook Pool gorge is deafening heard above the roar of the river, even half a mile away from the lodge at Salmon Hole pool.

When the rain in the mountain has stopped, the river recedes, as much as a foot every two hours or so, often back to normal in thirty-six hours. The salmon return from wherever they sought refuge during the deluge, perhaps in an eddy or protected from the swift current by a large rock. Invigorated by the aerated water,

Normal level at Salmon Hole pool.

Salmon Hole pool after hurricane.

they start rolling and jumping at intervals for reasons of their own. Often then they are more attracted by a properly cast fly.

It is only after experiencing such a "flood" spectacle that one can recognize the causes of and use for the vegetation-bare, wide smooth rock areas that line the riverside away from steep ledges and from side to side between the islands formed by the split river. The size of rocks displayed is determined by the speed and volume of water flow during the higher levels: the smaller rocks moved farthest, worn smoother; the large rocks often with craggy edges from recent breaks when finally rolled from a higher perch.

There is no limit to the size and shape of water-smoothed stones. They vary in color from black to white, yellows or striped, even to a pocket-size selection of heart-shaped stones picked up by a romantic lad, put in his pocket for his sweetheart back home.

The quiet flycaster may observe a muskrat, its furry head spearing a V trail on a quiet pool, or be surprised by the pound and splash of a beaver tail nearby. But he remains always alert for a prowling mink or silently cruising seagull capable of stealing a fresh-caught salmon or trout.

It is prudent to stay away from the river when spring rains raise the thick ice on the pools and it makes its way in fast water down the river. Few people have witnessed at close range the great chunks of ice riding the rushing high water to pile up in jams along the way, pile deep in self-made ice jams that are broken by pressure to surge again, the next crush of ice against a bank or curve, that too adding to the maelstrom. But scars left ten feet high on the trunks of huge yellow birches on the forested islands where the ice scraped the bark is proof enough that it was passing through and swerved too close.

How seeds and roots of the flowers of Arctic flora, miniature daisies and bluebells, can cling in a crack of ledge through such conditions is difficult to understand, but come spring, their flowers will bloom again.

32

Pools on the La Poile

By recent counts there are twenty-four named pools on the La Poile (see page 147). Though a wild, spirited river may at times eliminate the holding capacity of a pool—or eliminate the pool entirely, either temporarily or permanently—someone at one time or another undoubtedly caught a salmon in each of these pools. Within memory the unlisted pools of the eastern branch of the river were the main route of the migrating salmon. Now, with the exception of a few pools at the lower end, they are no longer used by the salmon. So, too, one may expect the major river flow to change back from the west to the east side of the valley at some later date. Every fisherman has a favorite pool. *His* pool as it were. It is not unusual with a party of six that if asked over eggs and bacon which pool each would like to fish, no two would choose the same pool. In fact, no one would skip a pool when fishing up or down river from the camp.

Some pools hold particular significance for individuals (or because of special memories) that warrant more than others to be described without discrimination against any not described. Certainly Salmon Hole Pool, commonly called the Camp Pool, is one of them. The beauty of the spot and its terrific upriver mountain view, coupled with its capacity for holding salmon, was recognized by Frederick Strickland at least before 1940, when he and others built the first log cabin camp on the high and flat west bank. The river bends and drops in a rocky hundred-yard-long slant eight feet or more from the Lower Salmon Brook Pool into a scramble of large rocks at the head of the Camp Pool, each rock forming a protective eddy where a salmon might rest before

Lower end of Camp pool.

Dunc's pool.

dashing through the fast-water stretch above. There is a high ledge bank on the opposite side from the camp. This marks a deep hole that the current has extended a hundred yards down the length of the pool to where it again breaks into a rapid, rock-strewn fall. The pool is wide, thirty-five yards or more along its entire length, running northwesterly to southeasterly. (Thus, it has more sunshine on fair days than the more northerly-southerly runs of other pools.) Salmon hold in the more aerated water at the head of the pool with water at normal height; at high water levels, however, they seem to concentrate at the lower end of the pool, though it is not unusual to see salmon jumping at both ends.

Upstream, a quarter mile above the original campsite and now the present camp, Salmon Hole Brook falls from the mountaintop into the lower end of the gorge of Upper Salmon Brook Pool. There is a substantial fall at the head of the gorge between huge boulders. The northwesterly side of the river is a steep, slanted ledge formation. Opposite is a steep rocks, brush, and tree-studded cliff. Just inside and before a sharp bend—opposite where the brook enters at the lower end of the fifty-yard pool—is the

High water at Salmon Brook-Bathtub pool.

Split Rock pool.

Bathtub, a pool within a pool, its name derived from the tub-shaped depression where salmon often hold. There is a narrow and deep gut where the river exits the upper pool to make its way to the long and wide lower section of Salmon Brook Pool. In late season, the sea trout wait in the deep water beneath the steep ledge-lined gut for budworms and hairy caterpillars that fall from the overhanging foliage. Though a difficult place to make accurate casts because of the gorge aspects and an affinity for upriver wind, both the Bathtub and farther up on the opposite ledge are favorite spots for experienced fishermen familiar with the area.

Dunc's Pool is located half a mile or so downriver from the camp site. It hugs a low ledge on the westerly side after falling through a narrow three-foot drop, then widens to ten yards during its forty-yard length. It is fished only from the rock-packed easterly side, the opposite side being too steep and tree covered. Its capacity to hold salmon changes often. Weather conditions during the spring runoff, when midpool or below may be gouged deeper or filled, affect its depth and water speed. But salmon

Duncan Smith at Dunc's pool.

Doctor's pool.

Lower Salmon Brook pool.

must pass through here to get upstream; and they often rest in the fast, deep water just below the pool entrance. Cold water from a nearby spring attracts trout to the back side of the pool when the river water is warm.

Split Rock is the obvious name for the pool below Dunc's and past Birch and Jerry's. One of the two large rocks midstream is split, leaving its two points pointing up. This pool, too, is subject to changes in what part and how it may be successfully fished. The river is pushed back to the far bank by the first large round boulder, then to the split rock a few yards below. Though the fall has been slight over the previous hundred yards, it appears speeded by the pressure of passing through the narrower area behind the boulders and results in deeper water back and below the split rock, often extending some distance downstream and around the rock. During low-water periods, the pool may be better fished from the back side; but with high water, the fish seem to hold around and behind the split rock or a distance farther down in the lower end of the pool. And once hooked, because of the varying currents and the location of the two boulders, and usually on a short line, the challenge is to keep the fish hooked long enough to bring it to net. Furthermore, one is often distracted at Split Rock Pool by moose or caribou that claim the area as a favorite crossing place.

No two pools are the same. From Muskrat to Twin, some eight miles apart, each pool has its own physical characteristics, and varies with different water levels and weather conditions, different views, vegetation, and size of rocks although each is in its own ever changing bed of rocks.

Tile Pool
North West Pool
Ernest's
Mud Bank
Russ's
Sid's
Reg's
Mudler
Wall Pool
George's
Split Rock
Jerry's
Dunc's
Cripple

Old Camp Pool
Lower End of Camp Pool
Camp Pool
Night Cap Pool
Bathtub
Upper Salmon Pool
Peter's
Foley's
Allen's
Mish Pool
Ledges Pool
Doctor's
Twin
Thunder

Upper end east side of North Bay River
(no pools now on bay end)

Wid's
Bud's
Bright
Andrew's

(Listed by guide Sid Chant)

Guide Sid Chant nets salmon for Dr. Strout at Camp pool.

33

Dinner at "The La Poile Hilton"

No two of the six regular salmon fishing parties that stay at Salmon Hole camp on the La Poile follow the same menu; but each meal is prepared by experienced chefs (the guides), who always earn high praise. Each party brings its own food, including enough to feed the guides—six days' worth of food for nine hearty appetites.

The day begins when those awake in the bunk room hear the chef for the day (the guides take turns) come into the kitchen, tread softly across to the woodstove, remove the stove lid and put in the prepared kindling and a couple of sticks of wood, the match sparks, the lid is put back on. Then four steps across the room from stove to sink to fill the twelve-quart agate-ware tea kettle with water, put it on the gas stove, and turn on the flame. Then the guide is out with towel over his shoulder to the outside washroom.

When he returns to fill the eighteen-inch iron fry pan with bacon and stir and refill the fire, the fishermen straggle out, taking their turn in the washroom, returning mostly to be in the way of the chef as he puts the crisp bacon in a paper-towel-lined aluminum kettle (the handle broken off), into the oven to keep warm while he toasts bread (homemade by Alec's wife) four slices at a time in a folding, two-handled, wire-mesh "toaster" on top of the woodstove, butters it, and piles it into a large aluminum bowl and stores it in the oven. By that time, hungry fishermen are waiting in line with their plates held ready for the eggs—delivered in pairs from the hot bacon fat "over light", "sunny-side up", or "wrecked" as requested. Tea bags have been added (measured by

Head Guide Alec Chant by the old log cabin.

the handful) to the boiling water in the agate tea kettle, and is poured into mugs by a fisherman "helper." Breakfast is over quickly, and they pull on their boots or waders, check their rods and flies, and are off for their favorite pools leaving the dishes to be washed and the floor swept before the guides shed chef duty and take up their nets to follow the eager fishermen.

Lunch is at about noon at the camp and everyone is on his own. The tea kettle is full and hot. The home made bread is sliced as only a Newfy guide can do it: by holding the loaf upright in his left hand, slicing with a long, sharp knife toward his chest and letting the thick slices slide off the blade onto a plate. Sandwich makings on the table include peanut butter, jelly, cold cuts with mayonnaise and mustard, pickles and olives, often surprises such as a watermelon or a fresh pineapple, and plastic bags filled with home made cookies. Then morning fishing experiences are exchanged, some flies are swapped, a line cleaned, a reel repaired, and onto the bunk for a midday rest.

Fishermen are often late for lunch or may skip it entirely; but seldom is a fisherman late for dinner at five P.M.

Chicken over coals on the river bank, 1981.

In Dunc's time, and that of the old log cabin with the bear-broken oven door, the chicken legs and thighs, the steaks, or trout or salmon fillets were grilled outside on the woodstove oven shelf, which was propped up on four corner rocks among those beside the camp pool, heated by red-hot charcoal briquettes beneath. The fishermen and the guides crouched on convenient rocks around the fire to partake of the meal.

Now, you wait with your plate before the sizzling gas grill on the camp deck ready to jab your steak when it is cooked to your liking. You then return to the camp table to retrieve hot potatoes, rutabaga, carrots, onion, and cabbage from the thirty-quart aluminum kettle at center table, still steaming, each vegetable having been added so that all are "done" at the same time. And always the hot mugs of tea. With the end of the click of forks as party members spear their favorite vegetables and fill their plates, a strange hush falls about the room, only an occasional soft spoken word is heard: "Salt," "Pickle," "Bread," and always those thick slices of that homemade bread.

The rib-eye steak and/or the chicken legs/thighs menu may be

New Lodge at Salmon Hole.

Whittled kindling dries overnight on oven door.

repeated during the week; but Thursday's special, corned beef boiled dinner, is worthy of cutting the leader to release a salmon to avoid being late for the meal.

Baked beans and hot dogs are the ritual Saturday dinner meal. The guide-chefs lay aside their culinary duties on Sunday to pack and transport the gear from Salmon Hole camp to North Bay where a roasted, stuffed turkey dinner is cooked, arranged, and served by Alec's wife, Eilene, during an en route afternoon stopover.

I often think that some of us make that extensive trip just for the scenery and the meals; and, as may occasionally happen on a fishing expedition, sometimes we do, with no regrets.

34

Above and Beyond

A Chapter by James Staples

The very idea of a trip to Newfoundland to fish for Atlantic salmon seemed above and beyond any fishing I ever imagined doing. I did do it, though, and from Salmon Hole camp, three miles up the La Poile River, above and beyond took on a whole new meaning.

There are three pools I think of when I prepare for fishing upriver from the camp. They do not include Salmon Hole, the Bathtub, Peter's, or Foley's or Allen's, all of which are upriver. To me, beyond means Doctor's Pool, Twin Pools, and the elusive (mythological) Thunder Pool.

I caught my second salmon at Doctor's Pool, and that has been my favorite pool ever since. On my first trip there, my brothers, Dan and Russ, each caught one salmon, though Sid, our guide, warned that he didn't believe we would take more than one fish from that small pool (I have seen more than one taken several times since). I caught my first fish by doing exactly what Sid advised; but the second one I caught by studying the pool and fishing it as I wanted.

It was in 1981, before the budworm and blowdown, and we had walked all the way in the woods on the left bank of the river. Russ, Dan, and I hurried to keep up with Sid for three miles or more. Suddenly, Sid turned toward the river, reached up into a tree, and pulled down a tea kettle. Within ten minutes the kettle was boiling. We each had hot tea and were ready to fish. Doctor's Pool has several spots that hold fish and they can often be seen from the big rock overlooking the pool. I don't remember who fished first; but Russ took pictures that showed I took my fish

Russ, Jim and Dan Staples with guide Sid Chant.

from the upper end of the main run. One doesn't get out a lot of line in a small pool, but sometimes it is a lot of work to keep a fish in the pool. Once I waited many minutes while my fish sulked behind a rock on the far side of the pool, and I remember Rick Stark once smoked several cigarettes there in a similar situation. I also remember taking one that had driven a companion to distraction by ignoring every fly in his fly box. While he was preparing for the hike back, I tried a potato bug (green gantrum) fly with most satisfying results (so deadly that year and never since).

Twin Pool is three or more miles beyond Doctor's Pool. There are really more pools than the two that give the spot its name, but those are certainly the most interesting. The upper is a deep boiling pot of a pool with no sensible, classic way to fish it; but if one drops a bug in the right spot, a salmon or trout will rise up from the chaos and inhale it. Once the hook is set, there is no way to go but downriver, down over the five-foot drop to the more spacious and calmer lower pool. It must be rough on the fish. The rocky scramble undertaken by the fisherman is not easy either.

The wide sloping ledges around the pools provide a handy spot for boiling up some tea and even frying a trout to build up strength for the long walk back to camp. Over the cup, there is always talk of Thunder Pool, another six miles beyond, as the pool to try "next year."

A salmon hooked in Lower Twin Pool also tends to head for the ocean, but the wide ledges are more accommodating for the fisherman, and the fish can usually be stopped before too many pools are traversed. At last, the fishermen head back toward the camp, dinner, and bed.

The day after a trip upriver from the camp seems a good one to rest a bit, fishing the nearby pools and having lunch on the deck overlooking the Camp Pool. Then my eyes stray to the wooded slopes and I wonder what it might be like above the confines of the steep, narrow valley. The hills drew me the first time I saw them. I remember speaking to one of the local boys staying at North Bay that first year. I pointed to the hills and asked if he had ever been up there. "Nope." Well, why not? I asked. "I knows better, I guess." Well, I didn't (and don't) know better and have taken many hikes up both sides of the river in the ensuing years. Sometimes I go just to explore and see the spectacular view; more often I take a flag and put it up on a pole high on the hill across the river from the camp. My dad once asked Alec what could be seen from the top of the hill. "The next hill," was the reply. And so it is, one hill after another. Where there is no rock showing, it is bog or shallow ponds, and sometimes short, scrubby fir and spruce so thick one could walk (wearing a pair of snowshoes) on top of them.

The deerflies are incredibly ferocious, but no bother to me if someone else is along; I seem to be the less tasty morsel. When I at last turn to look back, about four miles of river is visible. Like a tiny matchbox, the camp and all the pools are in miniature, and far down the bay the magnificent cliffs are an incredibly beautiful sight. It lifts the heart even more than just being on the river.

The trip down is just a bit harder in recent years. Blowdowns as a result of the disastrous budworm infestation have decreased the moose and caribou traffic and blocked their trails that once penetrated the hillside forests. It is still a whole lot easier coming down than the trip up, and once again there is supper and bed to draw me back from "above and beyond."

35

The 'Mish" and the 'En' Flat

Our boots were sinking ankle deep in the water while walking on what appeared to be a floating, living tangle of vegetation that included caribou moss, bake apple, pitcher plant, and Venus flytrap. There was also a line of twelve-foot naked poles that reached from side to side, (remnants of the Morse code line that originally provided telegraph service from La Poile to Grand Bruit) and a host of other roots and water plants before I realized what guide Alec meant when he said, "we'll take the shortcut across the mish on our way to Doctor's Pool." We would have called it a marsh.

The "mish" on the topographic map is an unmarked flat area (one hundred feet above sea level) approximately twelve hundred meters long and half as wide, running parallel to and thirty or so meters higher than the gorge on the southeast side of Salmon Brook Pool. Because of the brush and stunted trees clinging to the high ledge bank, it is not visible from the level of the river.

It offers an alternative route for a fisherman on his way to pools above the gorge, a choice between hopping from shelf to shelf on the steep, narrow, slanted layers of slippery ledge on the northeast side (when the river is not high enough to cover the unmarked trail) and taking the chance that the next step on the mish will not break through to a lake or quicksand below.

In a conversation with the river warden, Phil Bond, I asked where the "en flat" he had mentioned got its name. His answer: "Because it was where the old folks kept the 'ens' during the summer. " His response was of little help a until an understand-

Guides Reggie and Sid Chant bring the party trout catch to camp.

ing native explained. The same reason corrected my mistake of Max's wife's name (after fifteen years) from Elda to Hilda, and in the genealogy of the Taylor family correcting George Taylor Sr.'s wife's name from Anna to Hanna. When the letter H begins a word among the North Bay folks, it is always silent. The "En" Flat was a small, grassed over tidal island just across the river from the village where the poultry population and their eggs were given protection against the village dogs and other predators, yet allowed access to sand for their gizzards and the edible grass and insects to augment the table waste, fish viscera, and other food in their varied diet.

There seems to have been little influence in word pronunciation among the local population resulting from access to radio and television except in the younger generations. Not unlike the local accents and colloquialisms of U.S. southerners in eastern North Carolina and the Acadian population of Louisiana, these families and villagers have developed and retained a vocabulary and way of speech distinct to the area. For example, in repeating an airwaves weather report, a native says, "The weatherman wants rain for tomorrow."

To the average visitor, a group of natives in animated conversation may as well be speaking a foreign language. However, when a native chats with a visitor, the flow of words is slowed. Though spoken with unmistakable Irish and Scotch-burred accent, the words are fully understood and appreciated—that is, if one remembers the silent H.

36

Reminiscence

Some of those who left North Bay now return each summer, perhaps to renew the memories of their childhoods. Their small cottages are neat and clean and their lawns mowed. Piles of newly split firewood lie nearby. In afternoon and evening gatherings the older ones recall what it was like before the fire, before they moved away. They are still "doers," not just retired. Jack Farrell built a substantial thirty-foot motorboat in one of the remaining workshops finishing it in two summers. Percy Taylor takes his rod to the river to catch his limit of salmon, picks gallons of bake apples and partridgeberries, has a small garden. The three sons of Max and Hilda Strickland bring in, cut up, and split wood. And they still talk about the old days.

When I visited the Taylors one foggy July afternoon, their teenage granddaughter was standing on a kitchen chair replacing a newly washed curtain. Percy had gone down the bay in his outboard motorboat to find and pick partridgeberries. Violet was taking hot loaves of fragrant bread from the ovens and when they were safely on the counter and covered by a white towel, she returned to knitting a wool sock. She explained than the gray yarn was some that she unraveled from a comforter she had knitted years before, when she and Percy lived in the big house on the same spot as their present cottage. She had sheared the sheep and those of Ern Jones, carded the wool, and spun the yarn.

Recalling those sheep reminded her of the time a lynx attacked and killed one. Someone in the village—she could not remember who—shot the lynx as it fed on the fresh kill.

With a wisp of sadness crossing her face, she told of the death of a son only a few months old. It was midwinter, bitterly cold, the ground frozen under deep snow. The small body was kept frozen until spring and then buried in a small plot near where stood the house in which they first lived as newlyweds across the two flows of the split river, on the East bank at the head of the bay.

She recalled stopping the bleeding and then bandaging his hand when young Norman Strickland, her sister's son, cut off several fingers while using a table saw. And she quite proudly identified herself as one of the family of "medicine women" of North Bay that included Josiah's wife, Julia, Violet's aunt, and Esther, her mother, each familiar with the treatments of the usual sicknesses and accidents, and all experienced midwives as well.

Through the window facing down the bay, we saw Percy returning in his boat, the sound of the outboard motor first warning of his approach. He came in with his lard pail but half filled with partridgeberries.

With a little prompting from Violet and his granddaughter, Percy related going at age fourteen with his older brother for two weeks or more on mountain traplines. He got his first look at a train, the narrow-gauge railroad, that ran from Port aux Basques to Saint John's, from where the trapline crossed the mountain overlooking Saint George, many miles from North Bay.

Percy and Violet left North Bay after the fire and moved to Bathhurst, New Brunswick. They bought a house and lived there for nine years while Percy worked on fishing boats catching cod and lobster, and cut pulp wood; but then they came back "home" to Newfoundland.

The next day, during a rare Newfoundland afternoon of warm sunshine, the Taylors, the Jack Farrells, and Arthur Farrell with his daughter Verna and several younger family members got together. They sat about on lawn chairs and on the steps of the Taylor porch, just talking.

I intruded, or at least felt like an intruder, but some of the past recalled may have been at my urging and for my benefit.

Jack described his father, Josiah, in glowing terms and remembered Andrew Strickland as a "funny man," jovial, joked a lot, but could revert to the opposite if crossed. Jack was present on the occasion of Andrew's accident and described it, the detail obviously firmly imprinted in his memory. Jack left North Bay in 1965 and lived in Bathhurst, New Brunswick. After twenty-four years he returned to Newfoundland.

In his cottage later that day, Jack recalled that when a young teenager, he made a midwinter visit to his uncle Eugene, who was cutting trees upriver. Jack had taken his .22 rifle, hoping to shoot a rabbit or a ptarmigan. As he and Eugene talked, a game warden, followed by a dog, joined them. After a while the dog found an interesting odor in a nearby snowbank and dug out a sizable chunk of moose meat. Unable to find another rifle, the warden considered Jack the poacher and was about to arrest him when Eugene claimed the meat.

Another poaching story involved an unnamed native who had shot a moose in mid winter close to the trail leading from North Bay over the mountain to La Poile. Someone using the trail, probably not from North Bay, reported the kill and identified the poacher. When the bay ice melted, word was sent ahead and the magistrate arrived to call a hearing and take action against the perpetrator. The individual charged was well advised, probably by those who had partaken of some of the meat or participated in its transportation, and he attempted to learn verbatim his declaration of innocence. But at the hearing he became so confused that instead of declaring his innocence his "speech" came out, "I stand before you a guilty man, and furthermore we all know that no one saw me shoot that moose, then there were two heavy snowstorms a few days afterward that completely covered any of my tracks where the poaching occurred and so you cannot prove a thing and I rest my case." I was not told the results of the court appearance; but I expect that the individual involved and others who participated continued, when in need of meat for their families, to neglect to consider the local laws.

Arthur told me that his father, Eugene, served as a forester during the First World War and that he, Ernest Farrell, and Max Strickland served in World War II. He provided information as to locations of the pioneer village homes, and remembered that

Alex Strickland and Josiah Farrell connected the Drinking Brook by pipe to four of the homes in about 1948, their first inside running water. He also recalled that bricks for the chimneys were brought in from outside—no bricks made at North Bay.

Conspicuous by their absence from their cottages and the sawmill building for the first time in many years were Ernest Farrell and Max and Hilda Strickland. Since 1980, when I first came to North Bay and for some summers before, Ernest and Max spent summers at North Bay. Ernest, tall at five feet eleven inches, and Max like his grandfather Andrew a little over five feet six inches, spent many hours operating the huge one-cylinder gas engine-powered sawmill. They pulled the logs by rope over blocks of wooden rollers to inside the building and lifted them onto the saw table, moved them by hand through the saw again and again to produce boards of the desired thickness. Some of the logs were brought down tied behind the trailer that the guides used to transport the sportfishing party's equipment, some were floated downriver, and some were brought up the bay by customers as far away as La Poile. Ernest and Max used the same building, the same motor and saw, the same tools that were acquired after the 1953 fire. Many of the boards were used to build the cottages that replaced the big two-story houses of their parents, to build sheds, rowboats, and lobster pots.

Ernest was unable to come back in 1995 and 1996; Max didn't make it in 1996. Max retired a few years ago after more than thirty years as River Guardian.

While trying to organize my notes in the Scott cottage the evening before I left, the door opened and a girl stepped in. "I have no one to talk to," she announced bluntly. "Can I come in?" I had seen her playing Frisbee with other children on the lawns and watched as most afternoons they all waded the river to swim in the warmer water of a lagoon by the far bank. Kelly Strickland is the fourteen-year-old daughter of Jimmy Strickland, granddaughter of Max, and great-great-granddaughter of North Bay pioneer Andrew Strickland.

She sat across the table and I reviewed some of her family history much of which she had never heard. Kelly lives with her

Cottages of Max and Hilda Strickland (left) and Ernest Farrell (right).

Cottage of Andrew Strickland.

From right: Jack Farrell's wife, Jean Farrell, his sister Dulcie Farrell Taylor, and Violet Strickland Taylor.

From left in the sawmill: Arthur and Jack Farrell and Percy Taylor, 1998.

Cottage of Percy and Violet Taylor.

Cottage of Norman Strickland.

Cottage of Phil Bond.

parents and an older and a younger sibling in Petites, a small village near Rose Blanche of about fifty residents. "Mostly old," she said. There were nine children in the local school, none below the fifth grade. Kelly will be leaving Petites to go to school in Isle-aux-Morts in the fall leaving only eight students, most of them her siblings or double cousins. There are no preschool children at Petites: "Only one pregnant woman, and they are moving to Nova Scotia."

We talked until my guide (and cook), Garland Chant, returned from playing cards with Kelly's parents, uncles, and aunts. With the young people leaving Petites, it, like North Bay, will be deserted of permanent residents. And the situation is not unlike many of the larger villages, even La Poile, where there is nothing to keep the young people from leaving and never coming back.

North Bay, after one hundred years.

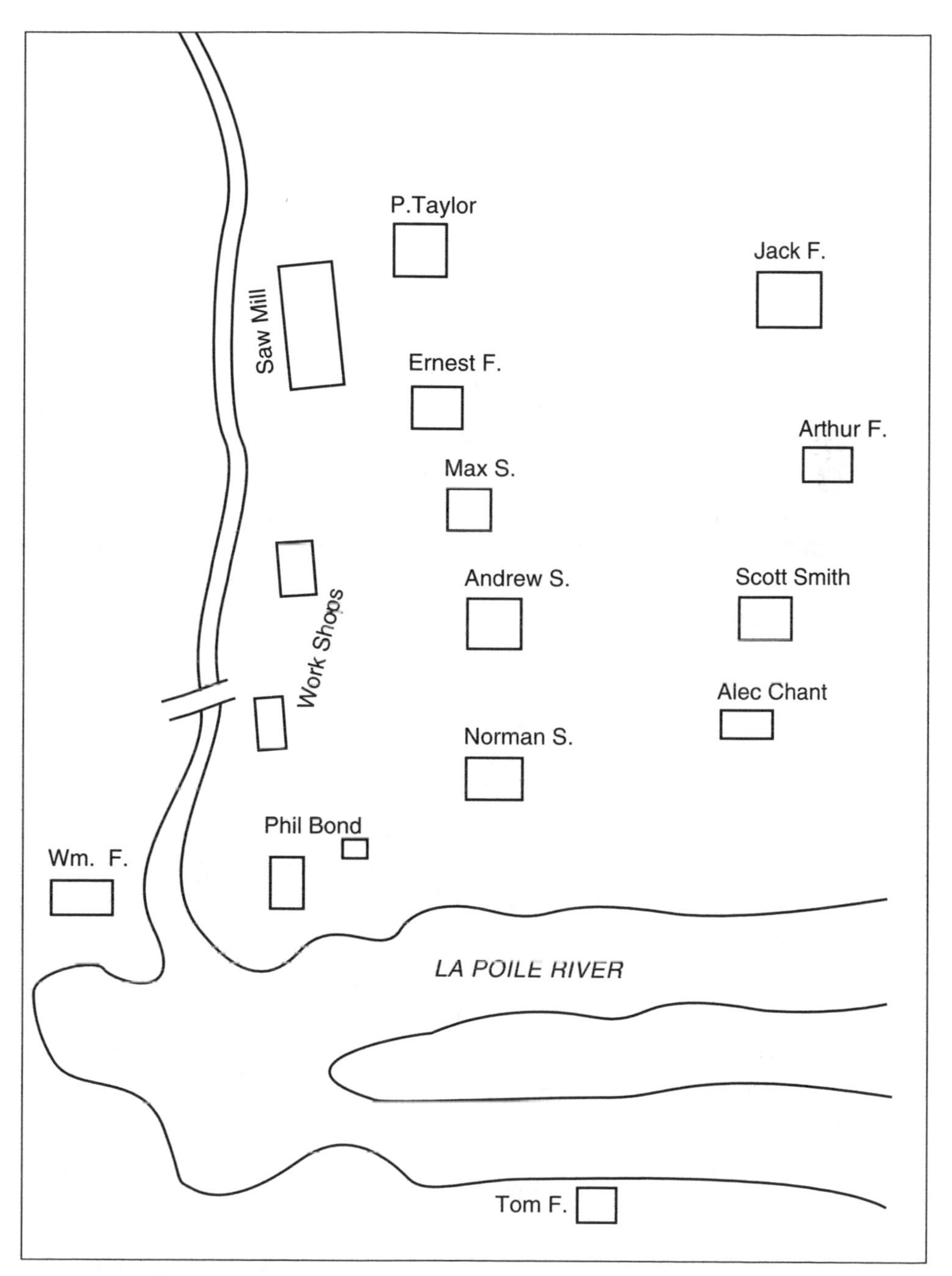

North Bay cottages, 1998.

Just Thinking

How lucky, how fortunate, can one be to have during his youth spent a summer with the famous and dedicated Arctic explorer, Donald B. MacMillan, cruising the coast of Labrador and Baffin Island aboard the fishing-racing Queen of the Gloucester fleet, the *Gertrude L. Thebaud,* captained by John Crowell, then in later years to have been able to extend those memories by being with the descendants of boat builders for the cod fishing fleet that once sailed that coast, and to have experienced nearly twenty years of annual trips fishing the LaPoile River in the valley rich in history of the pioneers who settled the rugged and remote coast of southern Newfoundland.

Words may describe the physical beauty of the area and sketch some of the individuals and their ways of living who pioneered those settlements when rowing, sailing of walking, often on snowshoes, were the only means of transportation; but words are utterly incapable of describing their inner thoughts and ambitions as children, adults, and senior citizens. The "diary" that Josiah Farrell wrote before he died was a proud record of his many accomplishments and of his leadership abilities. What would one have to do in our time to equal his accomplishments, and sorrows, and be as justly proud and satisfied with life?

As we pass through, or briefly stop, on our annual trip to Salmon Hole on the LaPoile, a moment, is well spent to reminisce perhaps "visit" one of the big, old houses at supper time, the long table well stocked with caribou or moose roast, or a codfish chowder, surrounded by children age one to twenty, always a blessing from the head of the table, heads bent in silence before the clatter of dishes and voices. Ninety years ago it was right there where Ernest Farrell's cottage, once the old village school, now stands empty; and where Drinking Brook enters the mouth of the LaPoile, an unfinished, fifty foot fishing boat is near to launching stage.

So few still live who remember North Bay as it once was, and too soon, even they will be gone.

Appendix

OWNERS OF ORIGINAL HOUSES AT NORTH BAY

When my grandfather's [Thomas Farrell's] house became empty, Percy Taylor bought it from Josiah and moved over to the North side of the river from the other side where he had lived, as he was mostly hired by my parents [Edward Farrell] and later worked for Jack Farrell when he [and cousin Arthur] took over his father's shops. It was nearer to his work and much more convenient for his several school-age children. Later, Percy sold the house to his brother George Jr. and moved to Petites. George Taylor Sr. always lived on the south side of the river. Max Strickland moved into Andrew's house after he got married and Andrew's wife had gone to live with a daughter. Frederick Strickland and Alex Strickland had built on the inside of the small stream that came down where the outhouses are. When Frank Strickland moved to Boston, he kept his house for a while so as to stay in when he came back to visit or buy lobsters; but Fred eventually bought and moved into Frank's house. Fred's house was small and he was at that time guiding fishermen and hunters and needed extra room to house them. [Fred sold to Duncan Smith and it was the last of the original houses to be torn down.] Alex Strickland bought Albert Strickland's house a year or so after Albert moved away.

Of all the two-story houses that were there, the original owners were Edward Farrell, Thomas Farrell, Josiah Farrell, Andrew Strickland, Frank Strickland, Albert Strickland, and Arthur Farrell on the west side of the river and Eugene Farrell on the east side.
—*Ernest Farrell*

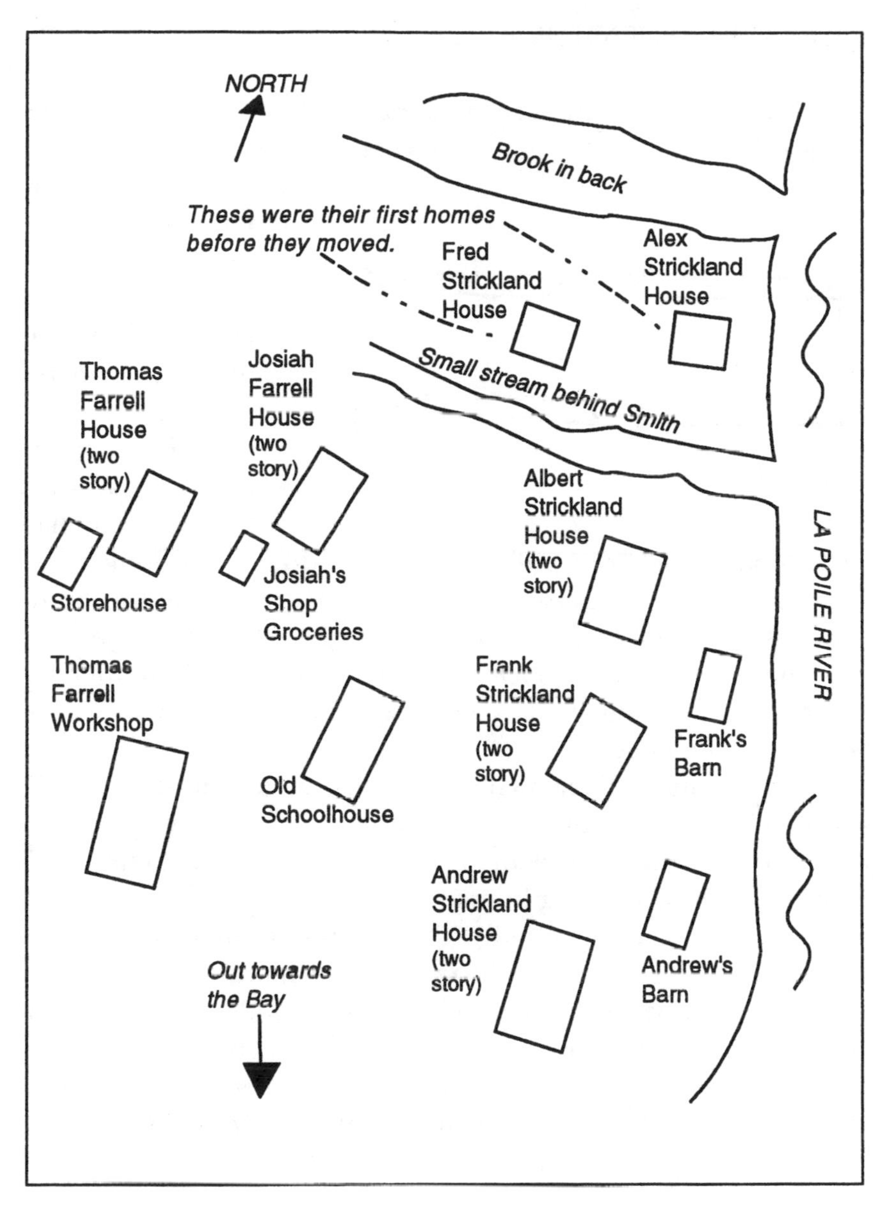

North Bay original houses.

NORTH BAY FURNITURE

A lot of the furniture was homemade. Most families had what they called "couches" [shown in diagram]. These couches and

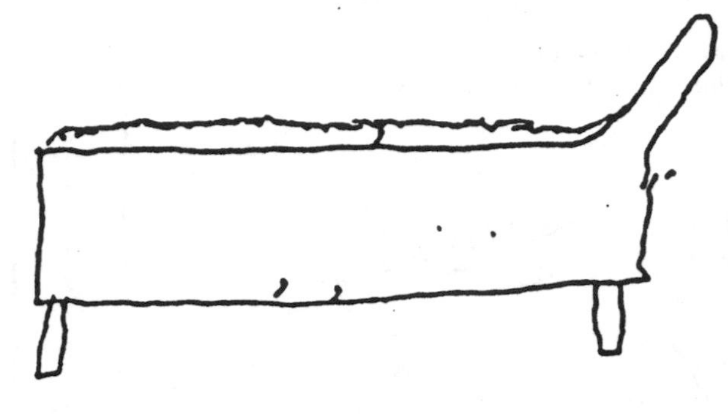

some of the chairs were homemade. In those days flour was bought in wooden barrels of size to hold 196 pounds. Some would cut them back to a desired height about half way around the barrel, put a seat in, and add rockers. Some made standard rocking chairs. They built their own tables. Some bought a few commercially built chairs, but most were made by the men of the house. Such furniture was worked on after the evening meal by the light of a kerosene lantern set on the home-made kitchen table.

Men also made their own snowshoes, under the same conditions at night or during a stormy day too severe for working outside. Edward (my father) and his brother Josiah each built a roll-top desk during evening hours.

The couches were stuffed with dry grass to make them more comfortable for resting or sleeping. The mattresses that were used on the beds were filled with feathers and were most comfortable and warm. All of the smaller feathers were saved when picking them from the birds, the larger feathers used in pillows. In those days, when I was growing up, it was "do or do without."
—Ernest Farrell

(Author's note: The passage of time and the lack of written records have prevented a more detailed genealogy)

STRICKLAND FAMILY

1st Generation

John Strickland (1852-?) m. Fannie Herridge (Morris) (1853-1939)
Alice, Andrew, Frank, John, Strickland, Loulea, Julia, Archibald, Rachel, May

2nd Generation

Alice Strickland (1874-?)
Andrew Strickland (1876-1943) m. Martha Taylor (?-?)
Frederick, Elsie, Harold, Albert
Frank Strickland (1878-?) m. Annie Farrell
Archibald Strickland (?-?) m. Minnie Farrell

3rd Generation

Frederick Strickland (1901-1973) m. Fannie Taylor (1900-1971)
Max, Elsie, Shirley, Ruby
Albert Strickland (?-?) m. Margaret Farrell

4th Generation

Max Strickland (1925-?) m. Hilda Strickland (?-?)
May, Andrew, Norman, James, Ruby

5th Generation

May Strickland (?-?) m. Chesley Frances
Kevin, Karen, Maxine
Andrew Strickland (?-?) m. Gladys Stagg(?-?)
Patricia, Amanda, Jody
Norman Strickland (?-?) m. Myrtle Stagg (?-?)
Harold, Kimberly
James Strickland (?-?) m. Bertha Stagg (?-?)
James, Kelly, Roxanne,

FARRELL FAMILY

1st Generation

Thomas Farrell (1859-1948) m. Elizabeth Strickland (1860-1921)
    Reuben, Josiah, Annie, Edward, Herbert, Sidney, Eugene, Minnie, Eva, William Farrell

2nd Generation

Reuben Farrell (1880-1973)
Josiah Farrell (1883-1974) m. Julia Stone (1890-1947)
    Minnie, Cecil, Dulcie, Leslie, Pearl Mildred, Edith, Linda, Jack
Annie Farrell (1884-?) m. Frank Strickland
    Marcie, Bessie, Edith
Edward Farrell (1886-1976) m. Annie Anderson (1893-1986)
    Ernest, Eva, Margaret, Patricia
Herbert Farrell (1888-?)
Sidney Farrell(1892-?)
Eugene Farrell (1895-?) m. John Strickland's daughter Bridget
    Arthur, William, Dora, Ronald, Gerald,
    Ralph m. Mary Taylor (?-?)
    Henry, Annie, Thomas, Rose
Minnie Farrell (1889-?) m. Archibald Strickland (1880-?)
Eva Farrell (1890-?)
William Farrell (1887-?)

3rd Generation

Minnie Farrell (b.1910)
Cecil Farrell (1914-1934)
Dulcie Farrell (b.1917)
Leslie Farrell (1915-1940)
Pearl Farrell (b.1919)
Mildred Farrell (b.1922)
Edith Farrell (b.1925)
Linda Farrell (1929-1995)
Jack Farrell (b.1927) m. Jean Billard
    Marcie, Bessie, Edith

Ernest Farrell (1913-) m. Judy Voutier (?-1996)
Eva Farrell (?-?)
Margaret Farrell (?-?)
Patricia Farrell (?-?) m. James Strickland

Arthur Farrell (1920-?) m. Mildred Billard (1924-1988)
  Patsy, Barbara, Loraine, Gordon, Keith, Verna, Lois
William Farrell (1923-1996) m. Lucy Billard
  Thelma
Dora Farrell (b.1924) m. Howard Boundy
  Harold, Robert, Joan
Ronald Farrell (b.1927) m. Beatrice
Gerald Farrell (b. 1927) m. Alice
  Eugene, Ronald, Christopher, Randy, Helen, Sharon
Ralph Farrell (1929-1990) m. Gertrude Reid
  Brian, Peggy
Henry Farrell (b.1936) m. Sussie Lushman
  Guy, Rennie
Annie Farrell (b.1940) m. Edward Ward
  Richard, Kevin, Karen
Thomas Farrell (b.1943) m. Maud Chant
  Daniel, Derrick, David, Dennis, Darline, Margo
Rose Farrell (b.1948) m. Wilfred Mauger
  Wilfred, Nicole
Minnie Farrell m. Archibald Strickland
Archibald Farrell (?-?)
Eva Farrell
William Farrell

4th Generation
Patsy Farrell(?-?)
Barbara Farrell (1946-1947)
Loraine Farrell (1946-1947)
Gordon Farrell (?-?)
Keith Farrell (?-?)
Verna Farrell (?-?) m. Vince Billard
Lois Farrell (?-?) m.

William Farrell (1923-1996) m. Beatrice
 Thelma
Dora Farrell (1924-) m. Howard Boundy
 Harold, Robert, Joan,
Ronald Farrell (1927 -) m. Beatrice
Gerald Farrell (1927 -) m. Alice
 Eugene, Ronald, Christopher, Randy
Ralph Farrell (1929-1990) m. Gertrude
 Reid, Bryan, Peggy
Henry Farrell (1936 -) m. Sussie Lushman
 Guy, Rennie
Annie Farrell (1940-) m. Edward Ward
 Richard, Kevin, Karen
Thomas Farrell (1943-) m. Maud Chant
 Daryl, Derick, David, Dennis, Darlene, Margo
Rose Farrell (1948-) m. Wilfred Mauger
 Wilfred, Nicole

TAYLOR FAMILY

1st Generation

George Taylor (1876-1963) m. Hannah Neil (1880-1962)

Eli (died young)
Fannie m. Frederick Strickland
George Jr. m. Louisa McDermott
Thomas m. Dulcie Farrell
Louisa
Mary m. Eugene Farrell
Jesse m. Reuben Skinner
Percy m. Violet Strickland
Ethel (died young)

2nd Generation

Fannie Taylor m. Frederick Strickland (see Frederick Strickland)
George Taylor Jr. m. Louisa McDermott (died in twin childbirth)
Thomas Taylor m. Dulcie Farrell
Louisa Taylor
Mary Taylor m. Eugene Farrell
Jesse Taylor m. Reuben Skinner
Percy Taylor m. Violet Strickland

3rd Generation

Percy Taylor (1920-) m. Violet Strickland

Evelyn
Audrey
Joan
Dorothy
Golda
James (Jimmy ?)
Wilson
Judy-Ann
Debby

STONE FAMILY

1st Generation

William Stone m. Charlotte?

- Esther Stone
- Julia Stone m. Josiah Farrell

2nd Generation

Esther Stone m. Henry Strickland

- Violet m. Percy Taylor (see George Taylor)
- Alexander ?
- John Robert ?
- Sidney ?
- Hilda m. Max Strickland (see Andrew Strickland)

North Bay Families with birth dates (about 1900)

Andrew Strickland (1876) wife Martha Taylor
Frederick (1901)

- Elsie Strickland
- Ethel Strickland
- Harold Strickland
- Albert Strickland

Frank Strickland (1878) wife Annie Farrell

- Marcie Strickland
- Bessie Strickland
- Edith Strickland

Thomas Farrell (1859) wife Elizabeth Strickland

- Reuben Farrell (1880)
- Josiah Farrell (1883)
- Annie Farrell (1884)
- Edward Farrell (1886)
- Minnie Farrell (1888)
- Eva Farrell (1890)
- Sidney Farrell (1892)
- Eugene Farrell (1894)
- William Farrell (1896)
- Herbert Farrell (1898)

NORTH BAY LAND GRANTS

According to Max Strickland (letter of 12/18/94), the following numbered land grants were made to Andrew and Frank Strickland:

> Number 10304, May 7, 1904
> Number 11658, Jan. 6, 1908
> Number 11660, Jan. 6, 1908

Jack Farrell, youngest son of Josiah Farrell, told me (July 1996) that his father had obtained several grants of small parcels of land including one up the river and one partway out the bay.

ABOUT FISH

I'd swap TV and radio
And cars and planes and railroad trains,
Give up baseball and skis and skates,
And briefly apple pie,
For rod and reel and floating line
And days on end where salmon run
Up tumbling rivers from the sea.
I'd skip the class where math is taught,
The junior prom and senior ball,
Stand up my date a second time
To spend the hours with casting rod
Or trolling on a rippled pond.

There is no way that fish can know
How many lives they save each year
Of men who are so overworked
But take the time to wet a line,
How many marriages are saved
Because the man can get away
And give his wife rest for a while;
Or how much money can be saved
If spent on lines and rods and reels
Instead of a psychiatrist.

The patience learned by fishermen
From salmon, perch and trout
Helps raise a family of ten
Or more or less as children come,
Helps teach the children patience too
So much we owe those little fish;
When telling of our fishing trips
We may exaggerate the fish.

Walter Staples

This is a diary of North Bay, Newfoundland

By Josiah Farrell

Author's Note: Josiah Farrell's "diary" provided an outline and helpful information that influenced me to write *The North Bay Narrative*. His daughter Pearl typed the handwritten diary and added a few pages. Ernest Farrell sent me a copy of the diary and furnished much more firsthand information, without which the book would not have been possible.

My father Thomas Farrell left West Point in 1892, and lived in Bay de East during the winter. He built a small house about a mile out the bay. He fished for cod and lobster. During slack season as it often was, he would build small boats, called row boats; these he sold at a dollar a foot. 10 ft. Keel $10.00 15 ft. keel $15.00. He built himself a boat 21 ft. keel, 7 ft. wide with two sweeps (long oars) 16 ft. long, and with nothing in it two men could row it along real fast; but when loaded it was much harder to move.

When fish was slack we (father and my brothers) would go to North Bay, cut logs, fill the boat, bring it home and start sawing plank, and material for the boats. (this was all done manually) the boats were not fancy but they were good strong seaworthy boats. When Reuben my older brother was home we sawed; when he left my younger brother Edward and I did the sawing.

Father kept a cow and some sheep. We had to go to North Bay to cut hay, dry it, and bring it home in the big boat then carry it to the barn. That summer father decided to build a house. He first built a store house, and moved the family in there while taking down the old winter house and building a bigger one. The house was 24 ft. long 16 ft. wide with a sharp roof. It was completed enough by fall to move in. The next spring Reuben went to Grand Bruit with John Chatney. $15.00 per month with room and board was the pay.

At this time there was one family living at North Bay: Mrs. Fanny Strickland, her two sons Andrew and Frank, also three daughters, Loulea, Julia, and Rachel; she had two other sons, one in Sydney And the other I'm not sure where.

Andrew and Frank bought a boat and decided to go coasting; They would be away months at a time. Their mother with the three daughters decided to leave. They sent for Mr. Squarey, the J. P., to measure the land in case they wanted to come back. Mr. Squarey came and was delighted with the place, told them they were foolish to leave as there was a good living to be made there. Frank, Andrew and Reuben with John Garson as Captain (he was former owner of the Bonnie) a 48 ton schooner in good condition, left to go coasting.

Mrs. Strickland and daughters went to Bay St. George's where she later married Mr. Morris. In later years he died and she came back to live with her son Andrew, she was always called Mrs. Morris.

Before Andrew left; he knew his mother and sisters would not come back unless there were other people living there; so he came to see father. I suppose he asked father to come live there, anyway the next thing we knew we were going to move. Father gave them the store that we had lived in while building our house, and he did not take down the new house he had built. Andrew and Frank gave him lumber to build at North Bay in return for the house he had already built. Andrew had a house partly built at North Bay. They had been living in a log cabin their father had built about 17 years before.

Once settled father started building skiffs, the first about 35 ft. on top, which he sold for $180.00. He had started another, I thought he was not getting enough for these boats so we agreed I would pay him $180.00 and take the skiff fit it out; and keep the difference, anything over 180.O0 was mine. It cost me $75.00 to fit her out; I sold her for $330.00 and made a profit of $75.00. I was then about 20 years of age, my brother Edward about 18; we all worked together.

After that Ned (Edward) and I started working on our own. We made our first model for a skiff. Mr. Herridge came from Harbour Le Cou. He used models to build, I showed him our model; he said "I believe she will sail", so we built one on it; it proved to be a good boat. We fitted her with sails etc. and we sold her for $400.00.

After this we started a small schooner 60 ft. long 16 ft wide; it needed 10 ft. of water when in ballast to float. In winter we went up river about 15 miles, to cut masts; The masts were 48 ft. long. We cut eleven, they were not all that long, main boom 40 ft. We made good time, was away four or five days. We had another young man with us to help pull them to the water, to float down the river; when he came home some one asked him how he liked it up there; he said he would never go back; it was worse than the war, at least there you sometimes had time to light your pipe, but up there you didn't.

We built and thought to sell her not rigged; but we couldn't so we had to rig her. The Stricklands had condemned the Bonnie that year, she had a new mainsail, and jumbo; so we bought her. Mr. Le Sellieur got a foresail and some blocks; we went to West Point and fitted her out. The first of August we left for Rose Blanche to have her measured; then to Channel where we had to wait for eight days to get papers. We got them and sailed for Sydney N. S. We ran into a heavy storm, gale winds S. E. rain and thunder; I asked the Skipper how she was lying to - he said very good, Next day we arrived in Ingonish. Next day to Sydney. We loaded and returned home. We did not contact anyone on the first trip. The second trip we left Rose Blanche with Charlie Clark's schooner, about 50 tons and another about 100 tons; one of R. Moulton's foreign going vessels. We kept close to the big vessel until she put up her light sails, then she went away from us; we only had the four lower no light sails; at sundown Clark was ten miles down to our lee quarter. When we left Sydney we were in company with another boat about our size, we skimmed past her. When we arrived Petites, there was a man waiting to buy our boat. So we sold her and went back to logging and building. The boat sold for $1100.00. By the time we had paid all expenses there was little left.

Sept. 1908, Ned was about 22 and I was 26; we came home and decided to settle down at North Bay. I got married 1909, started building, using a pit saw. We had never seen a saw mill but we knew the saw had to go round to cut and that it took power to drive it. so we started a water power. The stream was not very big, only enough water when raining or spring run off with snow melting.

We built a wooden shoot 420 ft. long 2 ft. wide and 6 in deep. The first axle we had made was 2 x 2 ft. We twisted that off before using it very long then got another 3 x 3 ft. that lasted longer; lots of times there was no water for power.

Ned and I worked together about twenty two years, and built 40 to 46 skiffs; most years we built two. We also helped start five skiffs for fishermen along the coast; we would do the frame work they would finish it. One was at Harbour Le Cou, two at West Point, one at La Plant, one at Grand Bruit. One at West Point was for Mr. Anderson and his sons. They helped us. We started Monday morning, Sat evening we put the rails on her. Someone told Mr. Scotty a boat builder at Channel what we had done, he couldn't believe it, said no ten men could do the job in that length of time. Our reply was, we did it and would not need him to finish.

After we had started building skiffs; John Moulton at Burgeo, a fish merchant decided to start building his own. He hired some men and started building. They built one; when it was finished Mr. Moulton said he could not get the material for what we were selling the finished product.

About this time we started a stationary engine mill. It was not long before we were turning out good lumber. I remember when we first started father was building a skiff and he needed some lumber for decking, jokingly I said wait until we get our mill going and we will saw it for you; he had never seen a saw mill either, and thought he would have to wait a long time, but with some help from Mr. Squarey it didn't take long to get going.

Frank Strickland had the first ox, the big problem was to fit the yoke. Ned had a young bull that he was using. Mr. Seeley a minister suggested using a horse collar; we were using the animals mostly on the frozen river. Soon the problems were solved and we were using oxen and bob sleds to haul the logs to the river. Then Frank tried his ox with pack saddle. I had Mr. Le Sellieur order one for me. He had it brought by schooner; cost $60.00 plus freight. It was a good beast.

November and December were usually spent working on

skiffs, we would put one sometimes two up in frame, then January and February we went up river logging. Usually we had one man to go with us. We cut 500 to 1,000 logs, one year 1,500. By March we were back working on our skiffs. At that time we had no sheds or work shops, and we would have to dig the frames out of the snow and get ready for the spring sawing (water mill). Mornings were usually spent on the skiffs. About noon when the water started to run we turned to the water wheel and sawing; quite often it was nine or ten p m. before we quit . This continued until the snow was gone, and the water run off. Once the mill was going we built a work shop, 69 ft. x 23 ft. Ned and I worked together about 22 years, and built about 46 skiffs.

As Ned had one boy of his own and one he raised, he decided to start on his own. I paid him his half of the stock so he built his own work shop, about the same size. In addition to the boats we built, we also remodeled a two storey house for a lady at La Plant, we also repaired a church at Rose Blanche the wind had moved. Ned worked for 20 years more building on his own. During this time he built twenty or more skiffs. Then he left home and moved to Ontario.

The time Ned started on his own my oldest son was about fifteen. So I hired Eugene, my youngest brother and sometimes Mr. Taylor. But I missed Ned helping chop the timber, and decided to try a band saw. I made the wheels and ordered nine saws. 3 - 1/2" - 3 1" - 311/2"; got it going, but didn't finish sawing one frame, before all the saws broke. I sent measurements of the wheels etc. pieces of the saws to Canada Saw Co. They told me the wheels were too small and the saw too thick; so I made more wheels about 3 ft. Diam. The saw was 14. ft. 8" Circum. I ordered 4 saws, these worked good; sometimes one would break but we could braize them. We built two ships most years, sometimes three. Mr. Debbin was the boat inspector and Mr. MacFarlane the supervisor in St. John's. Mr. Debbin told me one time he came that Mr. MacFarlane asked him "What is that man at North Bay building by steam?" Every two or three months he sends to me for another permit to build another schooner.

I worked building skiffs about 18 years after Ned started on his own, and in that 18 years I think I built at least 36 skiffs. That was up to 1946.

My oldest son died at the age of twenty. The next oldest son six years later at 24. In 1946 my wife died. At this time I told my other son Jack then nineteen, to take over. His cousin Bill who had been living with the family and working with us, would stay and work with him.

Later I built another smaller work shop, and built small boats (row boats). By 1966 there were only one or two families left. So I moved to Ontario too. Where I am at the present time.

Jack and Bill launched their first skiff in 1946. They built 9 in seven years. 1953 was the year of the fire, that burned all the work shops, machinery, tools, it also burnt the saw mill, one barn with an ox. But no one lost their home .

One thing, I will never forget. I had a cellar, dug in the bank near the saw mill, in front of the school. It had a wooden roof, covered with felt and tarred to keep out the water. A few days before the fire that roof blew off, we got it back in place, and a few days later it blew off again. In all the years it had been there it had never before blown off. The second time I said "leave it." If that roof had been in place at the time of the fire it would have caught fire, then the school and from there, my house and probably the whole village, the wind was in the right direction.

After the fire was out, it was a heartbreaking sight. No one knew what to do. They asked the Government if they would help. They wouldn't, except at 6% interest. To get engine, saw axle and belting would cost at least $3,000.00. To pay that money back, build the place up and live, looked a long hard road. So I told Jack if he wanted to start again I would help. So they started, and within one year they had everything working again. After things were going, Jack and Arthur started to build long liners. They built 6 in 10 years.

Things of interest.

School built about 1914.
Water Power about 1915.
Frank used ox first with pack saddle about 1916.
I think Ned had the first motor boat with 3 h.p. engine 1917.
Julie appointed Post Mistress 1934.
James Taylor mail carrier.
There were eleven families, at one time and from 45 to 55 people living there.
A skiff is a boat from 35 to 48 ft. overall and would be from 12 to 18 ton according to length.

Skiffs built at North Bay

Thomas Farrell	4	
Joe and Ned Farrell	46	
Ned Farrell	20	
Joe Farrell	36	
Alex Strickland	14	
Andrew & Frank Strickland	8	
Eugene Farrell	8	
Ern Jones	1	
Jack & Bill Farrell	9	
Jack & Art Farrell	6	long liners.
Bill Farrell	1	long liner.
	153	

Joseph's daughter Pearl added the following material:

This [Joseph's] story is very interesting and very accurate; but something is missing, the feminine side. These men were all real men, but the women were all women. They worked and worried right along with their husbands. My mother, Mrs. J. Farrell, was one of the very best; she worked, too, having to cut wood for the fire, carry water, washing on the old washboard. There were cows to be milked, sheep to look after, shearing in the spring the wool to be washed, carded, spun, and then the endless knitting.

I think the most dreaded thing was sickness, or accidents. The nearest Doctor was 75 miles by boat (no fast speedboats) when we were small, not any kind of motor; just oars to row or sails if the wind was right. Then there was no hospital; the nearest being North Sydney, N. S. another 100 miles by boat. But necessity is the mother of invention. Once Dad sawed his left hand, all four fingers, the little one fell over like a limp cloth. Mother stuck it back on, bandaged it and looked after it, and to this day it looks normal and healthy as any. The only reminder is a slight bend in the little finger that is barely noticed.

No one went to a Dr. or hospital for maternity; the midwife just came and stayed until another member of the family was welcomed. Dad must have been very disappointed on many occasions: girls and more girls, six in all, three boys.

During the time Dad and his brother were so busy building boats, the population was growing. Uncle Ned had married. He had four children, three girls, one boy, and another boy he raised that had been orphaned. Andrew and Frank Strickland had both married and had families; Dad's youngest brother, Eugene, married and settled there. Mr. and Mrs. Taylor moved there and raised their family. At one time there were ten or twelve families. By this time a school was needed. The government refused to pay to build a school; the parents supplied the lumber, built the school, and paid in hard cash for all school supplies so their children could have an education they had missed. Dad didn't have a so-called formal education but no one could beat him on figures, tallying lumber, adding up rows and rows of figures, he never missed. The government finally paid a teacher to come.

Thinking back, they were wonderful years. We were never without food, clothes, or a warm home. We had chores to do, which we did whether we liked doing them or not. It was always a real treat when Dad took time off every Christmas Eve to go with us to pick out and cut a Christmas tree and come home to a sparkling clean home with all the smell of Christmas goodies.

Children grow up fast. Some married and settled there. My oldest brother took sick one January. Everything possible was done but Mother soon realized he needed medical care. They took him at great risk to the nearest doctor, who realized there was nothing he could do: ruptured appendix. He died almost immediately. After that it was almost an epidemic in our family, eight out of nine had acute appendix operations at one time or another. The next oldest brother died at Sydney hospital after having his appendix removed. These were just a few of the family crises to arise in a lovely remote village.

The younger generation growing up had difficulties too. The men could always work along with their parents, but for the girls there was nothing. The oldest girl left home and traveled to Ontario, where eventually most of them came, married, and settled.

The Second World War had a greater effect on the village than the first. Several of the younger generation joined the services. By this time the timber situation was getting serious. All the continual cutting and no reforestation took its toll. To buy the lumber was too expensive, it would cost so much they just couldn't make it pay, so one by one the families living there gradually moved, helped of course by the new government's policy of moving smaller villages to larger places. Now it's a lonely lovely place where wildlife runs riot and the few houses, one being our original home and another our grandfather's home, still stand, looking lost and lonely among the trees and flowers that are run wild.

My mother died at the age of fifty-seven, just when she was able to relax and enjoy a few of the things she had worked so hard for. But time passes and life goes on. Dad eventually married again, and after a couple of visits to Ontario decided to live there, rather than live practically on their own so far away from medical care, etc. It's not the same but this new life does have its points, even if the good ones are more for us; being that we can see and visit whenever we take a notion, instead of having to travel so far. Our remaining brother is now in the mine drilling, living in New Brunswick. One sister lives in the Yukon Territory, the remainder of us in Ontario.

Dad went back once, about a year after he had left. It was rather heartbreaking, to know he was leaving, probably for the last time, a lifetime of work, home, property, just sitting. But it was not in vain. You left a lot of friends. Friends have memories, and memories, especially good ones, have a way of staying permanent, add nine children, seventeen great-grandchildren, and ten great-grandchildren, that's a lot of good memories.

GOD BLESS

About the Author

A native of Maine, Walter Staples is a graduate of the University of Maine. For 28 years, he traveled extensively in the United States, Canada, and Europe while engaged in poultry disease research for a major New England poultry breeding company.

His fishing experiences extend from catching trout in local waters to help feed a family of nine children to fly fishing for, and releasing, Atlantic salmon in New Brunswick and Newfoundland.

He has published numerous poems, short stories, and articles in newspapers and magazines. He lives in Tamworth, New Hampshire, with his wife, Virginia.